The Age
of Exuberance

BACKGROUNDS TO EIGHTEENTH-
CENTURY ENGLISH
LITERATURE

3 – 78, 110-121

skip 26-42

3 - 12

42-47

- 55

12-21

Studies in Language and Literature

The Age of Exuberance

BACKGROUNDS TO EIGHTEENTH-CENTURY ENGLISH LITERATURE

Donald Greene

University of Southern California

RANDOM HOUSE   NEW YORK

Preface

The aim of this book is to provide, for the student of English literature in particular, a guide to the salient historical, ideological, and aesthetic events and circumstances in Britain from the return of Charles II and the restoration of the "old constitution" in 1660 to around the time of the outbreak of the French Revolution in the 1780's. It was a crowded and complicated period of history; it is, moreover, a period which has been subjected to much misunderstanding and misrepresentation, which is only gradually beginning to be cleared away. The task, therefore, of trying to condense into a brief space all that ought to be said about it has been a more than usually frustrating one, and I must apologize for the many omissions and oversimplifications that necessarily result from such condensation. If I dare not say with Samuel Johnson, in the Preface to his great *Dictionary of the English Language,* "In this work, when it shall be found that much is omitted, let it not be forgotten that much likewise is performed," perhaps I may at least repeat H. L. Mencken's aphorism, when reproached for his amateurish but persistent piano playing, "If a thing is worth doing at all, it is worth doing badly"—better crudely executed music than no music. As a teacher I have often felt the need for some short compilation that my students could use in order to help them read the literature of the time with a better understanding of what its authors were talking about and of the assumptions they took for granted their readers would bring to it; and whatever the defects of this book, it is this need that I have had chiefly in mind as I put it together.

The title perhaps calls for explanation. When I was first exposed to the eighteenth century as an undergraduate, or earlier, the current custom of describing it as the "age of reason," or decorum, or restraint, or unemotionality, or "distrust of imagination," or "slavish obedience to rules" never made the slightest sense to me; it still does not. What attracted me to the century then, and what still attracts me, is the magnificent, apparently inexhaustible and indefatigable fund of sheer *energy* that its best art affords—the energy one hears in the firm bass line of a Bach allegro or the apocalyptic choral and orchestral climaxes of a Handel oratorio, that one sees in the fantastic design of a Vanbrugh mansion or the steeple of a Wren church, in the extravagantly imaginative conception of a great Reynolds portrait or a Nollekens bust, in a drawing room decorated by Adam or furnished by Chippendale, that one responds to—unless one's ability to read the plain sense of the words in front of one's nose has been subverted by dogmatic preconceptions about what one is expected to find there—in the *Walpurgisnacht* quality of *Mac Flecknoe, The Dunciad,* and *A Tale of a Tub* (Dryden, Pope, and Swift would have needed to take no lessons in "the literature of the absurd" from its twentieth-century practitioners; why should they, when they had all sat at the feet of its supreme exponent, Rabelais?), in the elaborately baroque diction and sentence structure of Johnson's *Rambler* prose style and the demonic hammer blows with which he demolishes a Lord Chesterfield or Soame Jenyns, in the fervent religious passion that shines out from the poetry of a Christopher Smart or Charles Wesley or William Cowper.

"Poetry," said Keats—we may expand it to "artistic creation" generally—"should surprise by a fine excess, and not by singularity" (by "singularity" Keats means what Johnson meant when he warned the poet not to "number the streaks of the tulip"); and "Its touches of beauty should never be half-way, thereby making the reader breathless, instead of content." The artistic masterpieces of the eighteenth century, as of other centuries, were never guilty of half-heartedness or the failure of nerve that recoils from "fine excess." And if one is looking for *a priori* sociological reasons why this should be so, one can find many in the social and economic history of the "age of expansion."

As to why the nineteenth century should have wanted to think of the eighteenth in the way it did, one can speculate endlessly. One reason was undoubtedly the normal rebellion of any generation against its "image" of its predecessor, in which any stick will do to beat a dog. It is now a cliché that Dryden, Swift, and Johnson had a great many attitudes and values in common, so much so that they have all been lumped together as "Tory humanists" or the like. Yet we find Swift bitterly attacking the Grand Old Man of his youth, his cousin Dryden; and Johnson, in turn, even though as a young writer he had paid Swift the tribute of trying to imitate his satiric idiom, was in the habit of expressing himself with considerably less than enthusiasm about Swift's outlook and achievements. Blake and Wordsworth seized on Johnson as the symbol of what they wanted to revolt from; yet if one can bring oneself actually to examine the evidence, one will find that Blake's views on morality and Wordsworth's on poetry are really not very different from Johnson's. And the great Victorians were to suffer similar injustice in their turn at the hands of the writers of the early twentieth century.

Another reason may be the rise of "Eng. Lit." as a school subject in the middle of the nineteenth century, when the reaction against the eighteenth, or its image, was at its height. The poor academic and journalistic hacks who prepared the first school textbooks of English literary history, needing material to present about the various "periods" they thought it necessary to divide their subject into and desperate for neat generalizations, picked up and passed on such nuggets of vulgar wisdom from the Dick Minims of their day as that the eighteenth century was excessively fond of generalizations. (If the reader thinks I am unduly harsh toward the pioneers of the academic study of English literature, he should spend an hour or two in a large library browsing through the early college textbooks of the subject, which appeared from around the 1840's to the 1870's. They are incredibly awful.) Once enshrined in a widely used textbook, such "knowledge" gets handed on from one textbook writer to the next, attains a prescriptive right to existence, becomes the basis of critical and academic empires, and requires a cataclysm to dislodge it.

Finally, if one wanted to indulge as freely in grandiose generalizations as nineteenth-century critics did, one could venture the suggestion, based on the fact of the sad decline of English music, painting, and architecture in the nineteenth century from the splendor of those arts in the eighteenth—their retreat from the boldly imaginative into the cautiously derivative—that Englishmen of the nineteenth century were in fact a little frightened of the audacity and exuberance of their predecessors, and at the same time (without, of course, being able to acknowledge it to themselves) a little ashamed of their own pusillanimity by comparison, and that they managed both to neutralize the danger and to assuage their own sense of inferiority by creating the preposterous fantasies about the eighteenth century that they did. Psychiatrists could adduce analogous procedures from case histories of father–son relationships. But no doubt a good modern nineteenth-century scholar would have no trouble demonstrating that I am here being as inaccurate and unfair about the nineteenth century as the nineteenth century was about the eighteenth.

Los Angeles   D. G.

Contents

ix

Contents x

✿ One

The
Country
and Its People

The Country

It is an old cliché, but one can hardly begin a historical sketch of Britain without affirming it: during most of the past two thousand years, the patterns of British political, economic, and cultural history have to a large extent been determined by the geographical situation of the British Isles in relation to the main routes of communication and trade of the European community and, later, its colonial extensions. During fifteen hundred of those years, from Julius Caesar's time down to Columbus's, the islands were on the fringe of that community, seldom closely involved in its affairs except when, as in the sixth to the tenth century, they found themselves in the path of migrating Teutonic tribes and Viking plunderers, and when, because of dynastic accidents, Norman and Plantagenet rulers led expeditions of military conquest back and forth across the Channel.

There was always some cultural and commercial interchange with the Continent; and missionaries brought the islands, like other outlying parts of Europe, into the orbit of Christendom. Yet the Channel always exercised a powerful isolating influence: Danes, Normans, Continental churchmen might come over determined to impose their ways of living, thinking, and talking on the islanders, but before many generations had passed, manners, ideas, and speech all took on an insular quality, and by the later Middle Ages had been blended

(in the most important quarter of the islands) into a self-sufficient Englishness that sometimes even became (in Church matters, for instance) defiantly anti-Continental. This insularity, or
independence, persists; and it is dangerous at any time for the
student to lump together English literary and intellectual phenomena with those of a Continental movement such as "the Enlightenment" or "Romanticism" without making due allowance
for the stubborn idiosyncrasy of the English.

But in the sixteenth century a fundamental change took
place. With the extension of Europe into the Western Hemi-
sphere, Britain found herself no longer on the fringe but in the
hectic center of international activity. British history during the
four centuries from 1500 to 1900 can perhaps be summed up as
the struggle of the British to come to some kind of terms with
their new position in the world—the struggle between, on the
one hand, the old "isolationism," the desire for self-sufficiency
and the stability that goes with it, and, on the other, the potent
attractions of world power, with its rewards, both material and
psychological, and its dangers, both economic and moral. (In
the twentieth century, the basic terms changed again; and in the
1950's and 1960's it has been the United States which, like Britain in the 1750's and 1760's, has had to face the challenge of
substituting an internationalist for an isolationist posture.)

For Britain, the struggle reached its climax in the middle of
the eighteenth century—specifically, in the Seven Years' War, of
1756–1763 ("The Great War for the Empire," as one of its most
eminent historians, Lawrence Gipson, terms it)—and its outcome, in the political and economic spheres at least, was a deci-
sive victory for expansionism over isolationism. The result was,
for better or worse, the great British territorial and commercial
empire of the nineteenth century; and the theme, explicit or
implicit, of a great deal of the serious British literature of the
time (not unlike that of serious American literature of the mid-
twentieth century) was the probable impact on the spirit of the
individual of this new affluent and *engagé* society. Yet, as perhaps the most acute contemporary observer of these events, Samuel Johnson, noted—in the opening sentence of a magazine first
published, under his editorship, in the month the Seven Years'
War was declared—"The present system of English politics may

properly be said to have taken rise in the reign of Queen Elizabeth." The controlling tendencies of political and cultural life in eighteenth-century England are merely a continuation of the tendencies whose power began to be felt in Renaissance England; but the pace becomes much more rapid, and the consequences, for good and bad, become more clearly discernible.

One of the most significant indications of what was happening to Britain in the eighteenth century was the striking increase in its population during the period. After centuries of a relatively slow and stable rate of increase, it suddenly became a rapidly expanding society. It began to experience a "boom," a "population explosion." The population of England (and Wales) at the end of the seventeenth century is reliably estimated at a little over 5 million—not much more than it had been a century earlier in the time of Shakespeare (in the densely populated world of the mid-twentieth century, we are always a little startled when we recall from what small groups of human beings the great artistic and intellectual achievements of the past emerged). At the end of the eighteenth century, however, when the first government census was taken (1801)—and it is significant of the changes that were taking place in ways of thinking that it was not until this late date, and indeed in the face of strenuous opposition, that the principle of taking a physical count of population was adopted—the figure had nearly doubled, to almost 10 million. This rapid expansion was to continue throughout the nineteenth century, when the population of the country quadrupled, and was to level off only at the beginning of the twentieth.

The causes of this phenomenon, as of many others in demography, are obscure, and most explanations of it are highly speculative. Since most of the increase seems to have taken place in the second half of the century, it is natural to connect it with the "Industrial Revolution," though why the many new factories that sprang up in northern England from 1770 onward should have found themselves automatically provided with a supply of operatives is hard to say. The thesis of one of the best social historians of the period, Dorothy George, is that for all the emphasis later placed on the miserable living and working conditions of the early years of industrialization—and they *were* miserable—they nevertheless represented an improvement over the way the masses had previously lived, and that the concern shown by men like Blake and the seventh Lord Shaftesbury for the workers in the "dark Satanic mills" is testimony of a heightened awareness for the lot of the poor. Earlier in the century this awareness had manifested itself in the organization of many charitable and welfare movements and in improved sanitary and medical facilities, and thus (around 1750) in a striking decrease in the death rate. Even Pope, that bitter satirist of the "degeneracy" of England under the regime of Sir Robert Walpole, conceded, in a complexly ironic epigram "on the large sums of money given in charity in the severe winter of 1740–1741,"

> "Yes, 'tis the time," I cried, "impose the chain,
>   Destin'd and due to wretches self-enslaved";
> But when I saw such charity remain,
>   I half could wish this people should be saved.

> Faith lost, and Hope, our Charity begins;
>   And 'tis a wise design in pitying Heav'n,
> If this can cover multitude of sins,
>   To take the *only* way to be forgiv'n.

Hogarth's "Gin Lane" gives a most horrible picture of the effects of the easy availability of cheap gin on the life of the poor in the early part of the century. But the many efforts made by Parliament under Walpole and his successors to enact legislation that would satisfactorily control the sale of liquor—never an easy task, as modern legislators know—are often forgotten. Several unsuccessful or only partially successful acts were passed before the really effective statute of 1751 was arrived at. The consumption of spirits decreased from 8 million gallons in 1743 to around 2 million in 1760. The Act of 1751, Mrs. George says, "was a turning point in the social history of London. . . . The measures to check excessive spirit-drinking had been forced upon the Government in the teeth of vested interests by a general protest in which the middle and trading classes had taken a leading part." [1] It also helped that about this time the price of tea (whose virtues were so stoutly defended by Johnson) dropped enough to make it available to the lower classes. But that there was no deficiency of "social consciousness" in the eighteenth century, a reading of the many essays in the *Tatler* and *Spectator*, the *Rambler* and *Idler* that deal with social abuses—imprisonment for debt, the tyranny of country squires, the hard lot of the prostitute—will readily confirm.

At the beginning of the eighteenth century, then, Britain was still a relatively small, isolated country on the fringe of the European community, which included such larger and seemingly more powerful nations as France (perhaps 16 million people) and Spain (around 10 million). Anomalously, however, she boasted the largest and wealthiest city in Europe—London, whose population, calculated to be 674,000 at the beginning of the century, considerably exceeded that of Paris, its nearest rival, and was many times that of Rome. The influence of London on English life was therefore strikingly great, all the more so since no other English town could come near to challenging its supremacy. The next most populous, the seaport of Bristol and the manufacturing town of Norwich, were each less than 30,000 at the beginning of the century. Toward the end of the century, Birmingham, Liverpool, Manchester, Leeds, and Sheffield were beginning to grow into the great industrial centers they became in the nineteenth century—but only beginning. Most of them did not send members to the House of Commons, nor, in the eighteenth century, was there any great agitation for their representation; this was not to come until 1832.

When by the end of the century the population of London had increased to nearly a million, agrarians like William Cobbett and Romantics like Wordsworth denounced the squalor, materialism, and crime rate of "the Great Wen," and deplored its baneful effects on the primitive virtues still preserved in rural England. (There has never been a time in English history when people have not looked back nostalgically to an earlier "Merrie England.") By this time London, like the similarly denounced New York in the twentieth century, was becoming not merely a national but an international capital; artists and intellectuals from other parts of the world—Voltaire (one of the earliest) and Rousseau, Mozart and Haydn, for instance—were beginning to feel the need either to visit it for at least a time, or actually to emigrate to it, Handel leading the procession that was to culminate in the next century with Karl Marx.

Most of the English population outside London lived in the agricultural south of the country; the great northward shift of the population, to the coal mining region, did not take place until the Industrial Revolution was well under way. The difference between country and town (i.e., London) life was striking, as the ecstasies of many a country wife in the comedies of the time when transported to town testify. Roads were abominable—it was thought a daring innovation when, in 1669, public coaches announced their intention of trying to travel the fifty miles from London to Oxford in one (long) day instead of the two formerly required—and were infested by highwaymen, many of them, like Macheath in *The Beggar's Opera,* glamorous public figures. Communications were difficult, and social amenities in the country limited: Zephalinda, in Pope's charming epistle "To Mrs. Blount on Her Leaving the Town after the Coronation," has to make do with a neighboring squire

> Who visits with a gun, presents you birds,

quail and pheasant that he had shot, most unenticing of gifts—

> Then gives a smacking buss, and cries—"No words!"
> Or with his hounds comes hollowing from the stable,
> Makes love with nods, and knees beneath a table.

In the rugged and sparsely populated north, life was more primitive still; it is seldom noticed even in the fiction of the time, though the bleak farmstead of Emily Brontë's *Wuthering Heights* probably represents north English life in the eighteenth century well enough. The north, to be sure, had scenery; but as has often been pointed out, mountains and deserted moorlands seldom provide much aesthetic appeal until the spectator has attained a way of life which makes them no longer hazards and inconveniences. The occasional *avant garde* intellectual, like that cloistered scholar Thomas Gray, might jot down some appreciative comments as he passed through the Lake Country (knowing that he would soon return to the comforts of Cambridge). But a good deal of Romantic propaganda was still going to be required before the delights of local Nature became viable to the average Englishman. Even then, Lady Louisa Stuart, Lady Mary Wortley Montagu's granddaughter, who lived through the "revolution in taste," had her suspicions that much of the ecstasy was affectation: "Can it be that the tastes and pleasures which we now esteem most natural are in fact artificial? What we have merely read, and talked, and rhymed, and sketched ourselves into?"

Politically, the British Isles in the seventeenth century were still fragmented into three nations. The official style of the monarch before 1707 was King (or Queen) of Great Britain, France, and Ireland. Wales had been incorporated in England under the Plantagenets, and given recognition in the title "Prince of Wales" bestowed on the monarch's eldest son. "France" was a relic from the time of Edward III, who had entered a hereditary claim to its throne; it was not, however, dropped from the royal style until 1801. Although King James VI of Scotland succeeded his cousin Elizabeth as King James I of England in 1603, and assumed the title of King of Great Britain, the two nations remained separate throughout the seventeenth century, the Scottish Parliament at Edinburgh legislating for the northern kingdom. By the Act of Union of 1707, negotiated with much difficulty by the English government (with the able assistance of Daniel Defoe), the Parliament at Edinburgh was abolished, and that at Westminster, to which a handful of Scottish peers and commoners were summoned, now legislated for the new nation of Great Britain.

Scotland, a turbulent and, by English standards, impoverished realm of a million or so people, had made trouble for its southern neighbor for many centuries, not excluding the seventeenth. One of the chief bones of contention had been religion, the Scots stubbornly adhering to the stern Presbyterianism introduced by John Knox in the sixteenth century, and refusing any hint of compromise with the episcopacy and liturgy of the Church of England. The great Civil War of the 1640's had been touched off as early as 1637 by Charles I's and Archbishop Laud's attempt to impose a prayer book on the Scots. In July of that year the initial "incident" occurred when, in St. Giles's, Edinburgh, the legendary Jenny Geddes hurled her stool at the officiating clergyman and cried "Will ye say Mass in my lug?"

An indispensable condition of the Union of 1707 had been the recognition of Presbyterianism as the form of the established (state) Church of Scotland, with the anomaly—to later eyes more than to contemporary ones—that the sovereign is head of an episcopal Church south of the Tweed and a nonepiscopal Church north of it. One of the most striking results of the Union was the beginning of that long southward procession of clever and ambitious young Scots whose finest prospect, Johnson grumbled, was the highroad that led them to England—Hume, James Thomson (whose patriotic ditty "Rule, Britannia" pointedly honors *Britain,* not England), Boswell, and many others.

John Bull's other island, Ireland, also furnished many brilliant men to the English intellectual community—Congreve, Swift, Goldsmith, Berkeley, Burke, Sheridan, to mention some. It had a larger population than Scotland (around 2 million), but, if its soil was more fertile, its economy was no more prosperous. Since the time of the Norman kings, the English government had attempted to keep Ireland in strict subjection, such as had never been successfully imposed on Scotland. It retained its own Parliament at Dublin until 1801, when a new Act of Union abolished it and transferred its powers to the Parliament at Westminster which, with Irish representation added to it, now legislated for the whole "United Kingdom," as the realm was then officially designated. But the Irish Parliament in the eighteenth century (in which of course only Protestants could sit) had strictly limited powers, and could pass only legislation approved by the English Privy Council. As a result, as Swift complained in bitter satires like *A Modest Proposal,* the economic needs of Ireland were consistently subordinated to those of England. Unlike Presbyterianism in Scotland, the Roman Catholicism of the vast majority of the (Celtic) population of Ireland received no official recognition and was, at best, ignored, and, at worst, persecuted; the whole population was required to pay tithes to the church of the minority, the (Protestant) Church of Ireland, which was closely affiliated with the Church of England.

As a result of these foolish policies, the history of the relations between England and Ireland for centuries had been one of intervals of ruthless oppression punctuated, whenever England found itself faced with difficulty elsewhere, by bloody insurrections—in 1641, at the outset of the Civil War; in 1689, at the time of the "Glorious Revolution"; and in 1798, during the French Revolutionary War—in which large numbers of the Anglo-Irish Protestant "ascendancy" were massacred. Fortunately for the eighteenth century, the years between the two last mentioned revolts were the longest period of peace that has so far endured between the two communities. The Celtic Irish, a half-starved and ignorant peasantry—"Teagues" was one of the favorite nicknames for them—were, for the English of the seventeenth century, objects of contempt, mixed with some fear; Dryden's pillorying of his enemy Shadwell under the name Mac Flecknoe is testimony of the attitude. Later the image of the "stage Irishman," the comic, hot-tempered, rather stupid, but good-hearted "Paddy" (like Sir Lucius O' Trigger in Sheridan's *The Rivals*) began to mitigate that attitude somewhat. But the sentimentalization of the Celt—the loyal and gallant Scottish Highlander as well as the warm-hearted Irishman—did not reach its full maturity until the days of Victoria.

For all that the two fringe regions of Scotland and Ireland remained remote, primitive, and somewhat ominous places in the mind of the average Englishman—though Samuel Johnson paid Scotland the compliment of a serious and thoughtful "socio-anthropological" study in his *A Journey to the Western Islands of Scotland,* 1775—it should not be forgotten that, as time went on, their capital cities became far from negligible centers of culture. Some of the finest city architecture of the eighteenth century is to be found in Dublin, and it was there that Handel (in spite of Swift's efforts to sabotage it) conducted the first performance of his *Messiah.* Toward the end of the century, Edinburgh produced an impressive group of philosophers and writers—a flowering sometimes termed "the Scottish Enlightenment"—and adopted the proud title of "the Athens of the North." Nevertheless, the intellectual and artistic life of the British Isles was overwhelmingly dominated (as it still continues to be) by London, and the nearby small but highly influential university communities of Oxford and Cambridge, much as that of twentieth-century America, in spite of its vast population, continues to be dominated by New York and its "suburbs" of Boston, New Haven, Princeton, and Washington.

The Monarchy

Then as now, the official structure of English society was py-ramidal, with the monarch at the top. It is well to point out, for the benefit of students brought up to think that the lively prop-agandist rhetoric of the American Declaration of Independence bears a close relation to historical fact, that England has always been a limited, never an absolute, monarchy. Macaulay summa-rizes it neatly: the royal power, he points out,

> was limited by three great constitutional principles, so ancient that none can say when they began to exist. . . . First, the King could not legislate without the consent of his Parliament. Secondly, he could impose no taxes without the consent of his Parliament. Thirdly, he was bound to conduct the executive administration ac-cording to the laws of the land, and, if he broke those laws, his advisers and his agents were responsible.[2]

Like the American Constitution, which is an offshoot of it, the old English constitution rested on the principle of the division of powers, the executive power being in the hands of the King and his appointed privy councillors (as with the President and his Cabinet), and the legislative power residing in Parliament, consisting of the King and the two representative Houses, the Lords and the Commons. For a law to be placed on the statute books, it must receive the assent of all three constituents (as, in the United States, of the President, the Senate, and the House of Representatives).

The great change in the British constitution by which, in effect, the executive and the legislative powers were transferred to the leadership of the majority party in the House of Com-mons, making the public actions of both the monarch and Par-liament usually no more than a formal ratification of what is decided beforehand in the Cabinet room, was not fully brought about until the mid-nineteenth century. Throughout the seven-teenth and eighteenth centuries, including the reign of George

The Houses of Stuart and Hanover (1603–1837)*

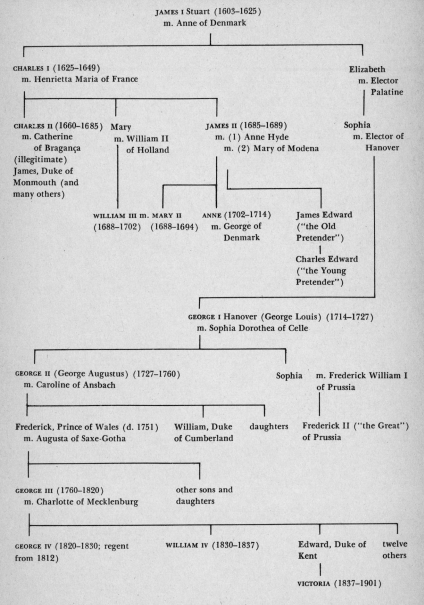

JAMES I Stuart (1603–1625)
m. Anne of Denmark

CHARLES I (1625–1649)
m. Henrietta Maria of France

Elizabeth
m. Elector
Palatine

CHARLES II (1660–1685)
m. Catherine
of Bragança
(illegitimate)
James, Duke of
Monmouth (and
many others)

Mary
m. William II
of Holland

JAMES II (1685–1689)
m. (1) Anne Hyde
m. (2) Mary of Modena

Sophia
m. Elector of
Hanover

WILLIAM III m. MARY II
(1688–1702) (1688–1694)

ANNE (1702–1714)
m. George of
Denmark

James Edward
("the Old
Pretender")

Charles Edward
("the Young
Pretender")

GEORGE I Hanover (George Louis) (1714–1727)
m. Sophia Dorothea of Celle

GEORGE II (George Augustus) (1727–1760)
m. Caroline of Ansbach

Sophia   m. Frederick William I
of Prussia

Frederick, Prince of Wales (d. 1751)
m. Augusta of Saxe-Gotha

William, Duke
of Cumberland

daughters

Frederick II ("the Great")
of Prussia

GEORGE III (1760–1820)
m. Charlotte of Mecklenburg

other sons and
daughters

GEORGE IV (1820–1830; regent
from 1812)

WILLIAM IV (1830–1837)

Edward, Duke of
Kent

twelve
others

VICTORIA (1837–1901)

*The student should familiarize himself with this genealogical table. Sovereigns'
names are in small caps; the dates are those of their *de facto* reigns.

III, the King was expected to be the effective chief executive of the country; though, as time went on and Britain became involved in increasingly extensive and expensive international activity, the cooperation of the House of Commons, which held the purse strings of the government, became more and more indispensable. When Johnson said, in 1772, "The crown has not power enough," he was not hankering after absolutism; he was merely complaining about a situation in which the central executive was hampered in giving strong direction to national affairs, as an American President might be when faced with a hostile Congress. Indeed, many seeming puzzles of eighteenth-century British political history become simple enough when translated into modern American governmental terms.

Still, within the traditional limitations of the constitution, there remained much room for maneuver, depending on the personality and ideology of the monarch (as there is in the American system, if one compares the history of, say, President Franklin Roosevelt's administration with President Eisenhower's). It was the genius of the Tudor monarchs that, without overtly infringing those limitations, they were able to create the strong central executive that Britain needed as it emerged from the medieval into the modern world. It was the misfortune of their successors, the Stuarts—at least, of three of them, James I, Charles I, and James II—that they lacked this kind of political tact and failed to heed the danger signals when they trespassed too blatantly beyond the traditional bounds. James I's bizarre treatment of his Parliaments laid the foundations of the scaffold on which his son Charles I was beheaded in 1649. But the fundamental strength and soundness of the old constitution was shown when, eleven years later, after hectic experimentation with various forms of republicanism, culminating in the only real despotism and dictatorship that has ever existed in English history, the English turned with relief to the restoration of the old system, and recalled Charles I's son, Charles II, from exile in France to take his place at the head of it.

The strictures on the political acumen of the other three of the first four Stuarts do not apply to the affable, cynical, and astute Charles II, who, having determined, as he said, "never to set out on his travels again," threaded his way with great skill through the complex and dangerous political mazes of his quarter century on the throne. In particular, his handling of the explosive crisis of the Exclusion Bill, 1678–1682, when it seemed inevitable that the Civil War would break out again in all its fury, was a miracle of political finesse. The British Restoration of 1660 is one of the very few restorations in history that have been successful—for contrast one may turn to the sad spectacles of the monarchist and Napoleonic restorations in nineteenth-century France—and the chief credit for its success must go to Charles himself. Victorian readers, accustomed to their historians' denunciations of Charles's private life, involving a dozen or so mistresses and innumerable illegitimate progeny (he "scattered his Maker's image through the land," as his loyal Poet Laureate, Dryden, wittily put it), must have been puzzled to find the rigidly moral Samuel Johnson praising Charles as the only English monarch for a hundred years who "had much appeared to desire, or much endeavoured to deserve" the affections of his people. But the praise was just.

As the personalities of the British monarchs of the seventeenth and eighteenth centuries (like those of American Presidents) had a good deal of influence in shaping the climate of opinion of their reigns, it will be well to devote some time to reviewing them. The Stuart family were an always interesting, often exasperating, and sometimes charming lot, more capable than any other dynasty that has occupied the English throne of arousing either fervent loyalty or violent antagonism. It has been suggested [3] that the key to an understanding of them is their more-than-average susceptibility to sexual feeling, sometimes overt, sometimes latent. Homosexual tendencies can easily be discovered in the biographies of James I, William III, and Anne; the heterosexual proclivities of Mary, Queen of Scots (James I's mother), Charles II, and James II were notorious; Charles I, after being dominated in his youth by his father's handsome favorite, George Villiers, Duke of Buckingham, was dominated in later life by his French and Roman Catholic wife, Henrietta Maria. Not, of course, that such susceptibility was unique to members of this one dynasty: from, say, William Rufus up to Edward VIII, certainly not excluding Queen Victoria, the sexual feelings of the English royal family have often affected the course of public affairs.

After the death of the popular Charles II in 1685, his near-fanatic brother James II, who, as Duke of York, had narrowly escaped being "excluded" from the throne on account of his religion, was forced into exile after three years of attempting the impossible feat of changing England from a Protestant to a Roman Catholic country. He was succeeded ("usurped," James's "Jacobite" partisans bitterly maintained), after the Glorious Revolution of 1688, by his dourly efficient nephew and son-in-law, William of Orange, Stadholder of Holland, leader of Continental Protestantism against the aggression of Louis XIV of France—like other Stuarts, worshiped by his supporters, execrated by his opponents. Associated with William III as Queen Regnant, though deferring to him in everything, was his wife, James II's elder daughter, the pious Mary II, who died of smallpox in 1694.

William was succeeded in 1702 by Mary's younger sister, "good Queen Anne," staunchly Anglican (but not very intelligently, as Jonathan Swift discovered), always under the domination of some more strong-minded woman—until 1710, of the famous Sarah Churchill, Duchess of Marlborough. Anne, married to the equally dull Prince George of Denmark, had numerous children, all of whom died young. After her death in 1714, the demise (succession) of the crown was controlled by the Act of Settlement, passed by the English Parliament in 1701 and still in force today, which provides that neither the sovereign nor his consort may be a Roman Catholic. Hence the crown went, not to James II's young son ("the Old Pretender"), who was brought up as a Catholic, nor to some fifty other Stuart descendants closer in birth, also debarred because of their Catholicism, but to the nearest Protestant heir, George Louis, Elector of Hanover in Germany, great-grandson of James I, and, as King George I, first of the Hanoverian line of British monarchs.

The Georges have always had a bad press among their subjects. A nineteenth-century wit summed them up:

> George the First was always reckoned
> Vile, but viler George the Second.
> And what mortal ever heard
> Any good of George the Third?
> When from earth the Fourth descended,
> God be praised, the Georges ended.

But the more closely one becomes acquainted with the early Hanoverians, the more one comes to see that they were very far from contemptible or negligible. On the male side, they were the representatives of the ancient German dynasty of Guelph, which in the Middle Ages had furnished emperors for the Holy Roman Empire, and, along with their opponents the Ghibellines, had given their name to a side in the great Italian Wars of Investiture. In the seventeenth century they had astutely promoted their Dukedom of Brunswick to an Electorate—that is, secured for the head of the family the much-sought privilege of being one of the nine great German princes officially charged with the selection of the Holy Roman Emperor; the title of Elector (*Kurfürst*) frequently proved the forerunner to that of King. They were popular rulers in their own dominions and were respected on the Continent as shrewd diplomats and courageous and efficient military leaders.

George's claim to the British throne came from the marriage of his father to Princess Sophia of the Rhine, sister of the daring Cavalier general Prince Rupert.[4] They were the children of James I's daughter, the beautiful and charming Elizabeth, the "Winter Queen" of Bohemia, whose husband's claim to that kingdom (as against that of the Catholic Habsburgs) had precipitated the Thirty Years' War, and who was therefore regarded by suspicious English Puritans as the one really staunch Protestant in the Stuart line. The Electress Sophia inherited her mother's brains and forceful personality, and, though an old lady, looked forward eagerly to becoming Queen Sophia I of Great Britain when her dull cousin Anne should die (she missed the crown by only a few weeks). Sophia was one of three generations of remarkably brilliant and intellectual women connected with the Hanoverian family; her granddaughter-in-law Caroline was the last of the group.

No court which maintained Leibniz as its librarian and historian and Handel as its director of music, as the Hanoverian court did at the beginning of the eighteenth century, deserved the sneers which the English bestowed on it. The fact is that a great deal of English hostility toward the Hanoverians stemmed from sheer provincial ignorance of the wider world of the Continent, even from philistinism (one thinks of Addison's, Swift's, and Johnson's sneers against the Italian opera introduced by Handel, chiefly because it was "un-English" and they knew nothing about it). Apart from George III, the British royal family from George I down to Edward VII has always had a cosmopolitan rather than a nationalist outlook,[5] and it annoyed the English greatly that the first two Georges did not seem to appreciate the great honor that had been bestowed upon them, but were always chafing to get back to their more congenial Continental dominions.

Sophia's son, George Louis, was fifty-four when he acceded to the British throne, and had earned a respected name for himself on the Continent as a diplomat and a general. It vexed his English subjects that he never took the trouble to learn their language. But he had no great need to; well versed in French, German, and Latin, and assisted by able and experienced Hanoverians, he was better able than his English ministers to handle the foreign relations of the country, and did so competently. The story is told of George's conducting in French a lively technical discussion of international affairs with an ambassador from the Continent, and from time to time tossing a perfunctory translation of the gist of it to his English Secretary of State, the Duke of Newcastle, who stood by fidgeting in uncomprehending embarrassment.

Unprepossessing in appearance and stolid in manner, except when alone with a handful of intimate friends, George made little attempt to ingratiate himself with his new subjects. Such social life as there was at court revolved around the Prince and Princess of Wales. The King's marriage to his cousin Sophia Dorothea had ended long before in an ugly scandal and divorce, and he contented himself with his homely mistress, Melusina von der Schulenburg, whom he created Duchess of Kendal,[6] and who exercised considerable political patronage. Like his son's, his interest in literature and painting was minimal; but (again like his son and many of his descendants) he passionately loved music, and stoutly supported his great protégé Handel against politically inspired attacks.

George Augustus (George II) was an impetuous, quick-tempered little man, who quarreled fiercely with his father—a habit of all Hanoverian heirs. But he was a courageous soldier (he was the last British monarch to lead his troops into battle, at Dettingen in 1743, a feat celebrated by Handel with a glorious *Te Deum*). In spite of his apparent indifference to intellectual activity, two great institutions of learning in his dominions were chartered by him and named after him, the Georg-August University of Göttingen in his Electorate of Hanover, and King's College, afterward Columbia University, in his Province of New York (his father had founded the Regius Professorships of Modern History at Oxford and Cambridge). Most important of all, he had the good sense to let himself be governed by his wife, Caroline of Ansbach.

Perhaps the most robust and brilliant intellectual who has ever occupied the British throne, Caroline's hobbies were philosophy and theology. She corresponded with Leibniz and discoursed with Joseph Butler, the most subtle English theologian of the century, whom she appointed her "clerk of the closet" (chaplain-in-chief) and whose promotion to a bishopric she arranged before she died. Her independence of thinking gave rise to rumors of her heterodoxy, even atheism, which her omission on her deathbed to receive the last Communion from the Archbishop of Canterbury did nothing to dispel. She was a plump, blonde, vivacious, outspoken woman, quite beautiful in her youth. Lord Hervey, whose memoir of her and George and their court is a literary classic, was obviously deeply in love with her; so was George Augustus, though he felt he owed it to his position as King to keep a series of mistresses, who, however, stood no chance against Caroline in his affections. Caroline was glad enough to have these ladies take George off her hands from time to time, for his company could be devastatingly boring (her daughters approved these tactics). But any of them foolish enough to embark on a trial of strength with Caroline regretted it, like Pope's friend, Lady Suffolk, to whom Caroline at last felt compelled to remark pleasantly that "it was in my power, if I had pleased, any hour of the day, to let her drop through my fingers—thus." Lady Suffolk soon left court.

Caroline loved power, and, working amiably and efficiently with her father-in-law's and husband's great Prime Minister, Walpole, exercised it competently for a decade. When she died in 1737 (of gangrene resulting from an untreated rupture of the womb, which she concealed lest it should diminish her attraction for her husband, and hence her power over him), George was heartbroken. Hervey recounts the wonderful scene when Caroline begged George, who was lying across the foot of her bed, blubbering uncontrollably, to marry again after she died. "Non—non," he sobbed; "j'aurai des maîtresses!" "Mon Dieu," Caroline murmured, "cela n'empêche pas." [7] (The anecdote shocked virtuous Victorians like Thackeray beyond measure.)

George, however, kept his promise and did not marry again, but immediately sent over to Hanover for his current mistress Amalie von Wallmoden (an action which shocked the virtuous Samuel Johnson) and settled down to another quarter century of uninspired but competent government, generally with the assistance of the Walpolian Whig "connection." The image he projected was anything but glamorous and when he died in 1760 at the age of seventy-seven, Johnson was not the only one of his subjects who felt, as he wrote to a friend, "We were so weary of our old King, that we are much pleased with his successor; of whom we are so much inclined to hope great things, that most of us begin already to believe them."

They were to be disappointed. "The young man is hitherto blameless," Johnson continued, "but it would be unreasonable to expect much from the immaturity of juvenile years, and the ignorance of princely education. He has been long in the hands of the Scots. . . ." The new King was George II's grandson, the twenty-two year old George III, son of the shallow-minded Frederick, Prince of Wales, who had died in 1751. Frederick had been the object of his parents' hearty detestation; at one time George II seems to have speculated on the possibility of separating his dominions, leaving Frederick to rule Hanover and putting his younger brother, the competent William, Duke of Cumberland, on the British throne. Young George III inherited Frederick's feud with both George II and his Walpolian Whig ministers and espoused the "patriotic"—i.e., anti-Walpolian—political line of the opposition, to which Frederick adhered.

Educated by Frederick's counselor, the Scottish Earl of Bute (whom political malice accused of being the lover of George's mother, Augusta, Princess of Wales), young George "gloried in the name of Britain" (not England), as he said in his accession speech; and, as if to point out the difference between himself and his two predecessors, he never set foot out of the country in his long life. His reign, ending in 1820, was exceeded in length only by that of his granddaughter Victoria. Faithful to his ugly wife, Charlotte of Mecklenburg-Strelitz, and father of fifteen children by her—one historian, J. H. Plumb, suggests that the strain and trauma of his connubial duties were a contributory cause of his periodic fits of insanity[8]—he settled down to provide his subjects with an example of bourgeois virtue, and as the simple, good-hearted "Farmer George" he was wildly popular with them.

The American myth that George was a ferocious tyrant has long been exploded by responsible historiography. He was an intensely conscientious and well-meaning individual, determined to fulfill his constitutional duties faithfully and for the good of his country, and to keep its government from being monopolized by coteries of grasping and self-seeking politicians. But he was highly neurotic, and, as Johnson said, immature and ignorant; and mere good intentions were inadequate weapons with which to counter the techniques of intrigue and propaganda used by such skilled practical politicians as John Wilkes and Edmund Burke, and, on the other side of the Atlantic, Sam Adams and Thomas Jefferson. He did much, however, to create —for better or worse—the twentieth-century British image of bourgeois and domesticated virtuous royalty. Unlike some of his successors in this tradition, for example, George V and George VI, but rather like such other historically unsatisfactory monarchs as Charles I and George IV, he was a dedicated and conscientious patron of the arts.

The Church

The elaborate organization of the Church of England was a heritage from the medieval Church, which showed a genius for administration that was in turn a legacy from the Roman Empire. It was Theodore of Tarsus, seventh Archbishop of Canterbury (668–690), born and educated in the Eastern Empire not long after the reign of that great administrator Justinian, who was largely responsible for imposing on the English Church the form of organization it retained in the eighteenth century (and still retains). The country was divided into some 10,000 parishes, each under a rector or vicar, which were grouped into twenty-six dioceses, each under a bishop. Four large but thinly populated northern dioceses constituted the Province of York, the remainder the Province of Canterbury, each with its archbishop; the Archbishop of Canterbury, as senior, held the title of Primate of All England.

The parish was the unit not only of ecclesiastical organization, but also of local municipal administration: the churchwardens and other officers of the parish were responsible for the levying and collection of local property taxes, including tithes for the maintenance of the church and the support of the parish priest, and their expenditure for local roads, the relief of the poor of the parish, and the like. The right of appointment ("presentation") of the parish priest was usually in the hands of the largest local landowner (formerly the lord of the manor), though it had sometimes been ceded to an Oxford or Cambridge college, or to the Lord Chancellor, acting for the crown. The nominee had, of course, to be approved of and formally "instituted" by the bishop of the diocese, but this was seldom refused; the right of presentation ("advowson") was looked on as private freehold property, and was jealously guarded. So was the right of the parish priest (the "incumbent"), once presented, to the fixed revenues allotted to him out of parish funds—hence such an appointment was called a "benefice" or "living." Once instituted, it was next to impossible to remove an incumbent against his will (it still is).

The bishops were (and are) appointed by the crown, on the advice of the Prime Minister. All bishops of the Church of England were spiritual peers, sat in the House of Lords, and took an active part in legislating, and sometimes political maneuvering.

Such an establishment was of course postulated on the assumptions that (1) England was exclusively a Christian country; (2) there is only one Christian church, the Church of England being a regional division of that universal (catholic) church; (3) there is no sharp division between Church and State, the function of government generally being to foster the welfare of the people of the country, spiritually and morally as well as materially. Indeed, in the Middle Ages, the civil affairs of the realm were often ruled by churchmen (as the best qualified administrators); bishops frequently held the office of Lord Chancellor, and the like. The last such appointment was made in the reign of Queen Anne, when John Robinson, Bishop of Bristol, became Lord Privy Seal.

These postulates had been accepted without question throughout Western Europe in the Middle Ages and beyond. But in eighteenth-century Britain the principle of the unity of Church and State was beginning to break down. The machinery of the fully established Church continued to operate (as it still does); the vast majority of the people of England formally adhered to the national Church; and it is clear that the assumptions underlying the establishment still appealed to "High Churchmen" like Swift and Johnson—and John Wesley. But the principle itself had been dealt a mortal blow by John Locke's *Letters on Toleration,* and by the Toleration Act, 1689, which for the first time recognized the legal existence in England of churches other than the national one. Both Locke's work and the legislation were the product of humanitarian and rationalist repugnance at the barbarity of the wars of religion, civil and international, that had vexed Europe for the past century and a half, wars stemming from the principle of *cujus natio, ejus religio*—all the citizenry of a state should be of the same religion. Locke's simple but powerful argument was that the use of force by the state to make men "true Christians" is itself a gross violation of Christian morality, an argument to which even conservatives like Swift and Johnson readily assented.[9] The Toleration Act did not extend its operations very far; it merely permitted Protestant Dissenters (not Roman Catholics) to hold their own services and attend them instead of those of the Church of England. But even to take legal cognizance of the existence of competing religions was looked on by many as a shocking innovation; and in the reign of Anne, the "high-flying" Tories, feeling that toleration had gone much too far, attempted to limit it again by the Occasional Conformity and Schism Acts. These, however, remained a dead letter. It was not until well into the nineteenth century, and only after much violent controversy, that Roman Catholics, Jews, and finally atheists were admitted to full civil equality. Even yet, the sovereign and the sovereign's consort are required by law to be Protestants.

In spite of the gradual decay of the *cujus regio* principle, religious loyalties and animosities were still responsible for many events in the political history of the late seventeenth and eighteenth centuries in England (and in the nineteenth, and even, in its relations with Ireland, in the twentieth). These often stemmed from bitter memories of persecution and aggression on one side or the other. Queen "Bloody" Mary I's burnings at the stake were only a little more than a century old at the time of the Restoration, and were vividly impressed on people's minds by John Foxe's *The Book of Martyrs,* sometimes kept in parish churches along with the Bible. Pope Pius V's excommunication of Queen Elizabeth, the descent of the Spanish Armada, above all the Catholic-inspired Gunpowder Plot of 1605, when Guy Fawkes was found ready to blow up the King and Parliament, were not quickly forgotten (an annual service of thanksgiving concerning the latter was incorporated in the Anglican Prayer Book) and still aroused fierce resentment and very real fear of the Roman Church.

Even more recent and vivid were the memories of the Puritan ascendancy of the 1640's and 1650's; not productive of so much bloodshed as the earlier Catholic activities—though the Archbishop of Canterbury, Laud, did lose his head—yet causing much misery to Anglican clergy evicted from their livings, and irritation to ordinary people through the closing of the theaters, insistence on the "Puritan Sabbath," and the like. About such "blue laws," the average Englishman probably thought much as Macaulay did: "The Puritan hated bearbaiting, not because it gave pain to the bear, but because it gave pleasure to the spectators." [10] And, naturally, Catholics and Puritans also remembered and resented what had been done to them when Anglicans were in power. These memories and resentments were potent political forces in Britain, from the time of the Clarendon Code of the 1660's down to the Gordon Riots of 1780 and beyond; especially so in bringing about the Revolution of 1689 and the settlement of the crown on the Protestant House of Hanover.

It is to the great credit of the leaders of the Church of England in the late seventeenth and eighteenth centuries that on the whole they steadily strove to diminish partisan animosity to other branches of Christianity and irrational exaltation of the status of the Anglican church. Such partisanship was to be found in the lower orders of the clergy—the rural parish priests who shared the isolationist prejudices of their patrons, the squires—and in a small but vociferous group of doctrinaire High Churchmen like Francis Atterbury, Bishop of Rochester, and Henry Sacheverell. But Atterbury was an appointment of the short-lived Tory ministry of the end of Queen Anne's reign, and few eighteenth-century bishops felt as he did.

Anne, curiously, was the only Anglican monarch (and temporal Head of the Church of England) for over a century, between 1649 and 1760. Charles II's conversion to Roman Catholicism was kept secret during his lifetime, but announced after his death. James II was a militant Roman Catholic. William III was a Calvinist, of the Dutch Reformed Church (his wife, Mary II, was Anglican, of course, but was guided by her husband in everything). The first two Georges were Lutherans. It was natural enough then that an ecumenical spirit should have prevailed among the crown-appointed hierarchy, although it was far from prevalent among the ordinary priesthood; indeed, the constant dissension between the two Houses of Convocation, the annual assembly of the Church—the Upper House consisting of the bishops and the Lower House representing the rest of the clergy—was such that from 1716 onward, the government refused to let it deliberate: another grievance, of course, for the more intransigent Anglicans.

The great Whig and latitudinarian bishops of the period have received harsh treatment at the hands of historians, who, for the most part, have followed the anti-Protestant line of the publicists of the Oxford Movement in the nineteenth century.[11] They have been accused of indifference and Erastianism and sloth for not taking a more militantly Anglican stand, for tolerating the encroachments of Dissent, and so on. In the ecumenical climate of the mid-twentieth century, however, it is difficult to condemn Burnet, Tillotson, and the rest for being too friendly to Presbyterians and Baptists.

The great scheme of "comprehension" sponsored in the 1690's by John Tillotson, William III's Archbishop of Canterbury, an attempt to broaden doctrine and ritual so that the Presbyterians and Congregationalists who had been ejected from the Church in 1662 might again join it, was easily sabotaged by Atterbury and the Lower House of Convocation; but the only objection that can now be made to it is that it was 250 years before its time. Not until the 1940's were serious schemes of reunion between Anglicans and other Protestants again devised, and, with the formation of the Church of South India, actually put into practice.

William Wake, Archbishop of Canterbury from 1716 to 1737, a fine scholar, was likewise concerned to establish liaison between his Church and French Huguenots, German Lutherans, and the Eastern Orthodox Church. Men like Edmund Gibson, Bishop of London, the astute administrator who was Walpole's right-hand man in ecclesiastical affairs; Joseph Butler, Bishop of Durham, a great theologian; George Berkeley, Bishop of Cloyne in Ireland, a great philosopher; such lesser but by no means contemptible figures as William Warburton, editor of Shakespeare and Pope and indefatigable controversialist, Robert Lowth, pioneer student of Hebrew poetry, Richard Hurd, a competent literary critic, Richard Watson, professor in turn of chemistry and divinity at Cambridge and a noted radical in politics, to mention some, make up an episcopate which compares very favorably in learning, piety, and energy with that of other periods. The eighteenth century had notable deans, too—Josiah Tucker, pioneer economist, for one; and Jonathan Swift for another. Queen Anne vetoed a bishopric for Swift; yet a Church willing to accept him even as a dean cannot be said to have been completely lacking in courage.

The lesser Anglican clergy were poorly paid and generally poorly educated by comparison with, say, the ministry of the Presbyterian Church of Scotland. To be sure, Fielding's Parson Trulliber and Parson Thwackum were exaggerations, as was Macaulay's "typical" Restoration country parson—

A young Levite . . . might be had for his board, a small garret . . . and might also save the expense of a gardener, or of a groom. Sometimes the reverend man nailed up the apricots, and sometimes he curried the coach horses. . . . He was permitted to dine with the family; but he was expected to content himself with the plainest fare. He might fill himself with the corned beef and the carrots: but, as soon as the tarts and the cheesecakes made their appearance, he quitted his seat. . . . Not one living in fifty enabled the incumbent to bring up a family comfortably. As children multiplied and grew, the household of the priest became more and more beggarly. Holes appeared more and more plainly in the thatch of his parsonage and in his single cassock. Often it was only by toiling on his glebe, by feeding swine, and by loading dungcarts, that he could obtain daily bread.[12]

But that such pictures could be drawn at all was the result of Henry VIII's confiscation of the endowments of the medieval Church, and the refusal of the economical Elizabeth to put it back on a proper financial basis. There has been much satire about the more enterprising individuals among the eighteenth-century clergy, who managed to get possession of plural benefices (though this, too, was a practice going back to the Middle Ages) and farm out their duties to young curates at a fraction of the income they received from them, or who, by judicious use of family or political influence, got themselves translated from a poor bishopric to a succession of increasingly well endowed ones. Nevertheless, the eighteenth century took the problem of the poverty and ignorance of the clergy seriously, and succeeded in doing something to remedy it. Queen Anne's Bounty, established in 1703, sought to supply the more than 5,000 parishes in England whose incomes were less than £50 with additional funds.[13] Energetic bishops like Gibson and Warburton insisted on careful examinations and adequate standards of educational preparation for their ordinands. In the latter part of the century, Johnson grumbled that bishops were now being appointed because of their social connections rather than their learning and piety, and it is true that a number of the bishops during this period were drawn from families of the nobility. Deplorable as this might be in itself, it nevertheless indicated a distinct advance in the status of the Anglican clergy generally; and at the end of the century Jane Austen—herself a daughter of the parsonage—can portray, what would have seemed astonishing to her master Fielding, such personable and intelligent young men as the Reverend Henry Tilney and the Reverend Edmund Bertram, and even make them the heroes of her novels; though to be sure there is also such a relic of the old regime as the Reverend Mr. Collins.

Was the condition of the Church of England generally stagnant, indifferent, secular minded, materialistic in the eighteenth century, as the standard histories of the period insist? Not extraordinarily so—no more than most churches at most times—as we are shown by the careful researches of Norman Sykes. There were slackers, certainly, as there will always be; but there were many other men in orders who took very seriously their duties of religious instruction and of setting an example to their flock; there were Parson Trullibers but there were also Doctor Primroses. The Communion was celebrated, children were prepared for confirmation, churches were built, sometimes as part of a governmentally sponsored church-building program—architecturally, some of the loveliest churches ever designed, products of the artistic genius of Wren, Gibbs, and Hawksmoor. The marriage laws were reformed (1753) to eliminate earlier scandals. Religious music flourished, both in the hands of great musicians like Purcell and Handel and in the humbler ones of hymn writers: the work of Watts, Doddridge, the Wesleys, Cowper, and others made the century perhaps the greatest period of hymnody in English history.

Of course any church, being an institution of fallible human beings, must always fall short of its exalted ideal. It is *semper reformanda;* and when reformers come along, it will be bound to have its shortcomings examined and condemned and to be exhorted to a higher standard of performance than in the past. The eighteenth-century Church of England was thus subjected to much criticism at the end of the century and the beginning of the next by two sets of reformers, the Methodists (and Evangelicals) and the men of the Oxford Movement. Given their position and their purposes, they were quite right to do so. But secular historians and their readers are not in that position. If the sincerity, devotion, and genuine religious conviction of the whole body of professing Anglicans of the eighteenth century are judged objectively, the period will not make a bad showing by comparison with many other periods in that Church's history, not excluding the twentieth century. Certainly the Church which nurtured laymen who took the fundamentals of the Christian religion so seriously as Johnson, Richardson, Cowper, Smart, Defoe, Steele, and Addison, to mention some literary figures, and Newton, Boyle, Locke, Handel, and Reynolds to mention some extra-literary ones, was somewhat more than moribund.

And the reform movements which produced such scathing criticism of the eighteenth-century Church were themselves, of course, a product of that Church. John and Charles Wesley were, like their inspiration William Law, Anglican priests utterly devoted to their Church, while determined to improve its effectiveness. They were all High Churchmen, a term which in the eighteenth century did not mean men with a leaning toward Roman Catholic ritual and dogma, but men who, like Johnson, felt that the Church should have an important and honored part in the life of the community. There was nothing particularly strange or novel about the Methodist or Evangelical movement of the eighteenth century: it was one of those periodic movements common to the history of Christianity in which a group of men feeling that the influence of the world has caused the Church to stray too far from its original ideals make an effort to return to those ideals. When the Wesleys, at Lincoln College, Oxford, in 1729, encountered Law's newly published *A Serious Call to a Devout and Holy Life*—young Samuel Johnson, a short distance away at Pembroke College, also read it and later reported that "this was the first occasion of my thinking in earnest of religion"—and decided to gather a small band of students to try to put Law's precepts into practice in their daily lives (and were nicknamed "the Methodists" by their fellows), their motives were not very different from those which in earlier times had actuated St. Benedict and St. Francis and Martin Luther and Ignatius Loyola—perhaps one may venture to say, which in the twentieth century actuated Pope John XXIII. The message of the Gospels must again be taken seriously, not allowed to become lost in a welter of man-made formularies and institutional red tape. Religion must be brought to the individual—to all individuals.

"The world is my parish," declared John Wesley, perhaps the

most authentic genius eighteenth-century England produced, and in his exuberance, determination, and almost incredible energy highly typical of his age. It was indeed the rigid medieval parish organization of the Church of England that defeated Wesley's efforts to reform the Church from within. Unable to bring his message to the great masses of uninstructed poor through that organization, he built up one of his own, an action which led in time to the separation of the Methodist Church from the Church of England, though Wesley always refused to regard himself as anything but a loyal priest of the established Church. (As this is written, the principle of reunion has been approved in England by both the Methodist and Anglican bodies. There has never been any doctrinal difference between the two groups.)

But the impact of Wesley on those who remained within the Church of England—the Evangelicals—was great. The seventh Lord Shaftesbury, William Wilberforce, the Stephens, Macaulays, Venns, and other members of the "Clapham Sect"—and their intellectual descendants of the Bloomsbury Circle in the twentieth century—were to become a potent force in keeping the Puritan conscience alive and effectively engaged for the betterment of English life. Even the Oxford Movement of the nineteenth century was to begin as an offshoot of Evangelical fervor, as the life of Newman testifies.

The Church of England, though by far the most important Christian body in the British Isles, was of course not the only one. The older English Nonconformist bodies, the Congregationalists, Presbyterians, and others, after a burst of activity following the ejections of 1662—the "dissenting academies" which they founded at that time, since only Anglicans could be admitted to Oxford and Cambridge, produced many notable men, including Defoe, Bishop Joseph Butler, and even an Archbishop of Canterbury, Thomas Secker—lapsed toward the middle of the century into comparative inaction, vexed with doctrinal disputes. The small English Roman Catholic body prospered under the ministrations of the energetic Bishop Richard Challoner and the growing spirit of toleration. In Scotland, the Kirk, the established (Presbyterian) Church of Scotland maintained its domination over the moral and, through the great Scottish universities and the admirable Scottish system of elementary schools, the intellectual life of the country. Here it was the Episcopal Church which was the dissenting and unprivileged body—a fact which explains Johnson's insistence, during his tour of Scotland with Boswell, on attending Episcopal and not Presbyterian services.

At the end of the century, however, it was through the Scottish Episcopalians that bishops were first consecrated for the Protestant Episcopal Church of the young United States. The failure of the rigid organization of the Church of England to supply bishops for the Thirteen Colonies—since, of course, its medieval founders had not contemplated its extension overseas—was perhaps one of the contributing causes of the breaking away of those colonies. The best it could do for the empire was the theory that all colonial Anglican churches came under the jurisdiction of the Bishop of London. The American revolt provided a salutary lesson, however, and before the end of the century bishops of Nova Scotia and Quebec, and, a little later, of Calcutta, were appointed. In Ireland, the anomaly continued of the elaborate organization of the established Church of Ireland, supported by public funds, ministering to the small Protestant minority of the population. Its top-heavy hierarchy—it had four archbishops, while the Church of England, with many times its number of adherents, had only two—furnished lucrative sinecures for relations of English noblemen and political friends of the English government. And yet the Church of Ireland nurtured many distinguished men: Swift, Berkeley, Archbishop King of Dublin, Archbishop Boulter of Armagh, and (a little earlier) Bishop Jeremy Taylor and Archbishop James Ussher. The Roman Catholic clergy who ministered to the great majority of the Irish populace were officially ignored, and their history has not yet been properly written.

The Peerage

The status of the titled nobility of Britain from the sixteenth century onward is sometimes misunderstood, especially by American students. It is quite wrong, for instance, to speak of

their "feudal privileges." The feudal power of the English nobility had been destroyed by the Wars of the Roses and the determination of Henry VII, the first of the Tudor monarchs, to
establish a strong central government for the nation without interference from private armies controlled by dukes and earls.
The English lords are "without vassals," Voltaire noted during
his visit to England in the 1720's—unlike the Continental nobles. A slight exception might be made for Scotland, where great
chiefs like the Duke of Argyll, head of the Campbells, and the
Duke of Atholl, head of the Murrays, could still rule their clans-
men despotically in the fastnesses of the Highlands.

But such horror stories as Dickens relates in *A Tale of Two
Cities* about the privileges of the French aristocracy before the
Revolution had been impossible in England since the Middle
Ages. Another important difference from the Continental system was the fact that the children of British peers are not nobles
but commoners—the children of the higher-ranking peers may
have courtesy titles but in law only the current head of the family is a peer. Whereas on the Continent (as readers of Tolstoy
will recall) the dozen offspring of a count are themselves all
counts and countesses, the younger son of the English Earl of
Blankshire is the Honourable Mr. George Smith, and his sons
are not even "Honourable." From shirt sleeves to shirt sleeves
(or commoner to commoner) in three generations is not the exception but the rule. Hence there has never been a closed aristocratic caste in Britain, and the British system of titles has en-
couraged rather than discouraged social mobility.

Very few English titles go back to the Middle Ages (that is, in
the family of the present holder; when an old title becomes ex-
tinct, it may be conferred, by a "new creation," on another family, to the confusion of the unwary student).* The Tudors
brought into being what was virtually a whole new peerage, to
reward useful political and other services to the central government, and many of the most impressively "ancient" English
noble families go back to some astute "operator" of the time of
Henry VII and Henry VIII. The fortunes of the Seymours,
Dukes of Somerset, the second senior English dukedom,[14] began

---

* The Note on Titles on pages 53–55 explains gradations of rank and
titles.

when Henry VIII's roving eye fell on pretty Jane Seymour, whom he made his third wife. Queen Jane produced Henry's only son. Thus her brother, the first Duke, was able to make himself Protector of the Realm when his young nephew, Edward VI, came to the throne. The Russells, Dukes of Bedford, and Cavendishes, Dukes of Devonshire,[15] descend from shrewd lawyers and land agents of that halcyon time of the real estate manipulators, Henry VIII's dissolution of the monasteries. The Churchills, Dukes of Marlborough, owe their position to the enterprise and generalship of John, the first Duke, and Sarah, his equally shrewd Duchess—and historians have not been lacking to accuse the Great Duke of some very sharp practice as he made his way up the ladder of success. The magnificent first Duke of Chandos, a possible model for Pope's Timon in the *Epistle to Burlington,* acquired his enormous fortune from his lucrative post of Paymaster to the Forces during the long and expensive War of the Spanish Succession, when, as the law then permitted, he pocketed for himself the interest on the vast sums of money held for payment of military expenses. The Grosvenors, Dukes of Westminster, got their start when a seventeenth-century Grosvenor married the daughter of a London scrivener, who brought as her dowry some large parcels of land which later became the most expensive real estate in the City of Westminster. Then, of course, there are the dukedoms which Charles II conferred on his numerous illegitimate children—Richmond, Grafton, St. Albans—the "sons of sons of sons of whores," as Pope elegantly designated their contemporary representatives.

Pope's language, published in a widely read poem, and Johnson's equally well publicized snub to the magnificent Earl of Chesterfield may impel us to ask just what the privileges of eighteenth-century noblemen were, if they were not immune to such insult. There were not many. There was the right to sit in the House of Lords and take part in legislation, a right which, as in the twentieth century, only a minority of the peerage normally took advantage of, generally men who had made politics their career to begin with and whose peerages had been conferred on them because of their success in it. Peers had the right, when charged with a felony, to be tried by their fellow peers rather than before an ordinary jury; and if found guilty of a capital crime, the right to be hanged at Tyburn with a silken rather than a hempen rope, as happened to the Earl Ferrers in 1760, when he was convicted of murdering his steward.

The fact is that the power of the peerage stemmed not from the rank itself, which was only a symbol, but, as with untitled men, from political success and the ability to accumulate money and property. Certainly it helped in Britain if one had been fortunate enough to inherit a viscountcy, just as in America it helps if one inherits the surname of Rockefeller or Kennedy and a share of the family fortune and influence—and acumen. But without these, the surname or the title would be of only limited assistance. There were playboy dukes and earls, descendants of men famous in British history, just as there have been playboy Astors and Vanderbilts. Pope scathingly catalogues some of them at the end of *The Dunciad:*

> The cap and switch be sacred to His Grace;
> With staff and pumps the Marquis lead the race;
> From stage to stage the licens'd Earl may run.

There were dukes whose chief diversion was to be amateur jockeys, and the current Earl of Salisbury, descendant of Elizabeth's and James I's great Prime Ministers, amused himself by driving the Hatfield stagecoach. On the whole, the situation of the inheritor of wealth and social position, whether or not graced by a hereditary title of nobility, was not very different in eighteenth-century Britain from what it is in twentieth-century America.

New peerages, then as now, were freely granted to men successful in politics and business, by governments that wanted their support. In particular, the most popular way for the poor but clever boy to make a name for himself in public life was through the legal profession. The eighteenth-century roster of astute lawyers of humble or mediocre origin whose success was symbolized by the acquisition of peerages is long: Lord Somers (to whom Swift dedicated his *A Tale of a Tub*); the Earl Cowper, the Earl of Macclesfield, the Earl of Hardwicke, the great Earl of Mansfield (who, however, was—unusually—the cadet of a minor Scottish noble family); Wedderburn, Lord Loughborough and Earl of Rosslyn; Lord Thurlow; Pratt, Earl Camden. The most striking instances were John and William Scott, sons of a very small tradesman in Newcastle, who became respectively the Earl of Eldon, the great reactionary Tory Lord Chancellor of the early nineteenth century, and Lord Stowell, eminent in maritime and international law. A later perennial Tory Lord Chancellor, John Singleton Copley, Lord Lyndhurst, was the son of the American painter, whose social credentials were minimal.

The military profession also provided a ready means of entry to the peerage for men sufficiently talented, and successful generals and admirals were so rewarded. ("A peerage or Westminster Abbey!" Nelson is supposed to have cried as he began one of his early naval engagements.) Anson, Hood, Howe, Collingwood, Gambier, Keith, Barham, St. Vincent, Ligonier, Amherst, Clive, Marlborough, Wellington are some names of naval and military peerages that come to the mind. Another group in the House of Lords who did not represent a hereditary caste was the twenty-six bishops and archbishops of the Church of England (the spiritual peers). Few of these—at least, before the middle of the eighteenth century—came from families of wealth and position, but rather had made their way by their scholarship and brains—and often, of course, through good luck in finding an influential patron.

A significant attempt was made in 1718 to block this free entry to the peerage. The Tory regime of the last years of Queen Anne's reign had ingeniously forced an unpopular statute through Parliament by promoting, at one blow, twelve of their supporters to peerages, thus securing a majority for the measure in the House of Lords. After the accession of George I, a large number of Whig peers were created; and in order to perpetuate their advantage, one group of Whig politicians introduced a Peerage Bill which would have placed severe restrictions on the number of new peerages the King could create. If it had passed, it would have drastically changed the whole character of the peerage and the position of the House of Lords. But it was defeated, and the peerage continued to be an open-ended institution. Even so, because of the predominance of Whig administrations in the early part of the century, the peerage tended for a time to become something of a closed corporation, the preserve of the Walpole–Pelham–Newcastle–Rockingham–Fox Whig faction, which was the party of the wealthier dukes, marquesses, and earls, such as Burke's patrons, the Duke of Richmond and the Marquess of Rockingham.

Toward the end of the century, however, this "Venetian Oligarchy," as the Tory Disraeli was later to dub them, was rudely shaken. The total number of peers at the beginning of the eighteenth century had been around 150; it remained at almost the same figure in the middle of the century. By its end, however, the number had almost doubled, to around 275. This was the result of the deliberate policy of the younger William Pitt, Prime Minister from 1783, with the hearty cooperation of George III, to crush the "old Whig" domination of the Upper House, by flooding it with newly ennobled lawyers and businessmen willing to support Pitt. Snobs like Jane Austen's Sir Walter Elliot grumbled about this. But the rising middle class (like Jane Austen's two brothers who rose to distinction in the naval profession) approved, and gave Pitt their firm political support. In short, the British peerage in the eighteenth century, as in the sixteenth and the twentieth, was rather a minor political phenomenon than a significant social one.

The Country Gentlemen;
the Agricultural Revolution

If a peerage was generally testimony that its holder or some not very distant ancestor had been one of "the new men"—a clever operator in business, land, or politics, or a professional man whose talent or luck had enabled him to climb the ladder of success—those who considered themselves the genuine old aristocracy of England, the backbone of the nation, the true hundred-per-cent Englishmen were the "gentry." This "squirearchy," proud of the plain designation of "Esquire," or, at most, "Baronet," the hereditary knighthood introduced by James I, lived on manorial estates which had been in the families for innumerable generations, perhaps even since William the Conqueror's *Doomsday Book*—not the huge estates, scattered over several counties, that the wealthy capitalists who acquired dukedoms and marquessates invested in, but relatively small tracts, where the squire and his lady could still take a personal and paternal, and sometimes dictatorial, interest in their tenants' doings.

Even as late as the twentieth century, heads of such families proudly refused to accept peerages offered to them by a government anxious to secure their political support. When they deigned to play an active part in national politics (though they were usually very active in local politics) it was as "Tories"—a word which in the terminology of the eighteenth century was not very different in meaning from the American "Independent"—refusing with equal pride to commit themselves permanently to the support of one or another of the warring Whig factions at Westminster. When one of them, growing bored with the delights of merely local power, did so commit himself, accepting office or a peerage from one of the government potentates, he was written off contemptuously by his former friends as having now become a "Whig." *"Renegado,* one who deserts to the enemy, a revolter; sometimes we say 'a Gower,' " Johnson wrote in the first draft of his *Dictionary,* referring to a Staffordshire magnate, formerly Tory, who had accepted the office of Lord Privy Seal in a Whig ministry, and whose descendants were to become Marquesses of Staffordshire and Dukes of Sutherland.

One of Macaulay's most amusing and memorable passages in the famous Chapter Three of his *History of England,* "The State of England in 1685," is that in which he describes the squirearchy. He stresses their parochialism, ignorance, and crudeness:

> Not one in twenty went to town once in five years, or had ever in his life wandered so far as Paris. Many lords of manors had received an education differing little from that of their menial servants. The heir of an estate often passed his boyhood and youth at the seat of his family with no better tutors than grooms and gamekeepers. . . . His chief serious employment was the care of his property. He examined samples of grain, handled pigs, and, on market days, made bargains over a tankard with drovers and hop merchants. . . . His oaths, coarse jests, and scurrilous terms of abuse, were uttered with the broadest accent of his province. . . . The litter of a farmyard gathered under the windows of his bedchamber, and the

cabbages and gooseberry bushes grew close to his hall door.
. . . Strong beer was the ordinary beverage. . . . The coarse jollity
of the afternoon was often prolonged till the revellers were laid
under the table.

No doubt there is some truth in this, but it is after all an account written by a violent Whig about a group which was consistently anti-Whig, a city-bred intellectual writing about the
country, a genteel Victorian shuddering at the vulgar physical
pleasures of a coarser age. Macaulay rather gives himself away in
a footnote where he refers the accuracy of his description of the
country gentleman "to the judgment of those who have studied
the history and *the lighter literature* of that age." Certainly the
loutish squire was a familiar stereotype for the comic dramatist
and comic novelist from Ben Jonson's Kastril, the Angry Boy,
up through Sir Wilful Witwoud, Sir Tunbelly Clumsy, Squire
Trelooby, and others, to Goldsmith's Tony Lumpkin and beyond. Fielding's unforgettable Squire Western probably contributed more than any other single source to Macaulay's portrait.

Fielding too was a Whig, an urbanite, and the cousin of an
earl; and the name of his great creation was intended to remind
his readers that Cornwall, Devonshire, Somerset, and other
western counties, heavily overrepresented in the House of Commons by comparison with other sections of the country, were the
stronghold of Toryism properly so-called—the politics of the
country gentlemen. The West, along with the North, had been
the chief source of Charles I's support in the Civil War, as
against London and the East, the center of Parliamentary and
Puritan strength. Cambridge, in the East, was always the Whig
and Puritan university; Oxford, toward the West, the Tory and
High Church one.

Of course the position of the country gentry was not so simple
as Macaulay described it, and it became more complicated as the
eighteenth century advanced. It is true that there were squires
as ignorant and brutal as those invented by the dramatists and
novelists. For the existence of one of them we have the testimony
of Samuel Johnson, a staunch Tory, but, being an intellectual,
one who wore his Toryism with a difference. This was Sir Wol-
stan Dixie, fourth Baronet, of Market Bosworth, Leicestershire,
in whose home young Johnson spent a few miserable months

when a master at the local grammar school, and whom he later pilloried as Squire Bluster in *Rambler 142.* His chief sports were tyrannizing over his tenants and quarreling with his neighbors. The story is told of his being received by George II, who, wanting to demonstrate his knowledge of English history, remarked, "Bosworth? Big battle there, wasn't it?" "Yes, your Majesty," the baronet replied, "but I thrashed him."

By contrast one may look at Joseph Wright's fine portrait of the elegant and sensitive Sir Brooke Boothby, sixth Baronet, of Ashbourne, Derbyshire, reclining on a grassy bank with a book of poems in his hand (perhaps his own, for he wrote poetry). Johnson was intimately acquainted with his family also—indeed, he may have been in love with Sir Brooke's aunt, Hill Boothby, who had a formidable reputation for learning and piety, and have wished to make her his second wife. The life of their circle is described in Richard Graves's novel *The Spiritual Quixote,* and in its earnest intellectualism and high seriousness is more reminiscent of the Bloomsbury of the 1920's than of Squire Western's abode (though even there, one remembers, Miss Western, the Squire's sister, was a great "politician," and prided herself on her expertise in national and international affairs).

And the more the political structure of England in the seventeenth and eighteenth centuries is studied, the more complex the political position of the squirearchy is seen to be. If in the time of Addison and Fielding it was possible to characterize their stronghold, the western counties, as the center of Tory reaction and isolationist resistance to Whig enterprise, it was also the West which not long before, in 1685, had been the scene of the disastrous uprising against the Catholic James II under the Protestant and "Whig" leader Monmouth, Dryden's Absalom and Shaftesbury's cat's paw. The role of the country gentry in bringing about the great Civil War has recently begun to be stressed; two of the greatest figures on the rebel side were country squires, Hampden and Cromwell, who, as Marvell said, cultivated

> . . . his private garden, where
> He lived reservèd and austere
> (As if his highest plot
> To plant the bergamot).

The controlling political principles of the squirearchy through-out the two centuries may be summed up as suspicion of almost any central government at Westminster as the source of foreign involvements and the wars that went with them, defense expenditure and the taxes that went with it, and general interference with the individual; and a reluctance to see agriculture displaced in favor of commerce as the staple of the English economy.

Like most other branches of the English economy during the eighteenth century, agriculture, which supported the gentry, generally prospered, even though commerce and industry caught up with it and surpassed it. There were ups and downs; there was the occasional bad harvest, with consequent distress, and in the late 1730's and early 1740's, and again in the 1750's, periods of genuine agricultural depression. Nevertheless, by comparison with the Continental nations, Englishmen in the eighteenth century were well fed and proud of the fact. Fielding's ditty achieved almost the status of a national anthem:

> When mighty roast beef was the Englishman's food,
> It ennobled our hearts and enriched our blood;
> Our soldiers were brave, and our courtiers were good.
>   Oh, the Roast Beef of Old England,
>   And Old England's Roast Beef!

Hogarth illustrated the point of view in his "Calais Gate," where thin, miserable Frenchmen stare longingly at a great rib roast borne on an Englishman's shoulders. English farms were able not only to feed and clothe the native population but to provide grain and wool for export throughout the century: Arthur Young, writing in the 1760's, reflects complacently on the fact that France has at last followed England's example and for the first time has permitted the export of grain for revenue, with a resulting stimulus to its production—"That nation [England]," he says, "became *great* from their exportation of corn."

And during the century, agriculture, like manufacturing, profited greatly from the general spirit of enterprise and the application for the first time of scientific thought to the problem of increasing production. Some of the leading figures in this "agricultural revolution," as it has been called, were Walpole's brother-in-law, the second Viscount ("Turnip") Townshend, who, after quarreling with Walpole and retiring from politics, devoted himself to encouraging the cultivation of root crops to provide fodder for cattle and swine during the winter months and so make serious mixed farming possible; Robert Bakewell, who initiated the scientific breeding of good strains of farm animals; Jethro Tull, whose influential *Horse-Hoeing Husbandry* (1733) advocated intensive tillage of the ground (to keep down weeds) and the rotation of crops; Thomas Coke of Holkham, Earl of Leicester, who vastly improved methods of estate management. Although the enclosure of small, uneconomical tracts and unproductive commons so as to form fields of large acreage had begun long before, it went on at an increased rate in the eighteenth century, to the accompaniment of Goldsmith's memorable lament in *The Deserted Village*.

What was happening to English agriculture in the eighteenth century was what happened to North American agriculture in the twentieth—the change from farming as a means of scanty subsistence for single families (in effect, a peasantry) to farming viewed as an industry and run on businesslike lines. The result in both cases was a great increase in total productivity, a great decrease in the number of individuals engaged in production, a consequent great shift of population from the countryside to the towns, and general social dislocation. Small tenant farmers and their families were uprooted from their ancestral acres and forced to take employment in the new factory towns or to emigrate. Absentee landlordism increased, as the owners of landed estates were tempted to leave their management in the hands of trained farm managers (stewards) and to seek the more stimulating atmosphere of London. This, in turn, meant the beginning of the end of the gentry as a separate political force: "Toryism" in the old seventeenth- and eighteenth-century sense was to die out in the early nineteenth, much as the not dissimilar Populism of agricultural America was to die out in the twentieth because of a similar shift in social and economic conditions.

All this, however, was perhaps not such a tragedy as Goldsmith thought, or thought he thought. When he wrote his poem, it had been many years since he himself had actually lived in "sweet Auburn," and he at no time demonstrated any great urge to give up London and the society of Johnson, Reynolds, Burke, and the rest to return to it. (Nor did the new class of urban factory workers. Whatever their grievances, as Marx himself pointed out, their lot was at least a cut above the stultification of the farm laborer's life.) The problems of a largely urbanized nation are many and have not yet been completely solved; but once the process has begun, there seems to be no turning back, and in the twentieth century the United States and the Soviet Union are having to face those problems which England, first among the great nations of the world, began to encounter two centuries ago.

The Business Community; the Industrial Revolution

A comic stereotype as popular as the boorish country squire in Restoration and early eighteenth-century literature was the money-grubbing businessman, the "cit," the bourgeois—Pinchwife, Alderman Gripe, Pope's Balaam in the *Epistle to Bathurst* —whose headquarters was the "City" of London, the old square mile that is still the financial district of the metropolis. His usual role was to be swindled and cuckolded by some gay young "wit" of the "Town"—Westminster, the West End, the seat of the Court, government, the professions, fashion, the arts. There was something more in this plot than merely crude humor: Wycherley, Pope, and the others did sense a threat to traditional moral and cultural values in what they saw as the increasing domination of English life by material and commercial values. It is the natural and proper outcome of the cit's blind devotion to financial success that his pretty wife, whom he has married as a status symbol, should be bored by his intellectual and emotional emptiness, and yield herself to the penniless but lively young "wit." [16] It was not forgotten that the City had been strongly Puritan and Parliamentarian in the Civil War; and Dryden savagely lampooned the London businessmen who had supported Shaftesbury and Monmouth in the struggle over the Exclusion Bill, those who "Adored their fathers' God, and property," and, like Shimei,

> Did wisely from expensive sins refrain,
> And never broke the Sabbath, but for gain.

But there were literary defenders as well as attackers of the new capitalism, and they were effective ones—Addison, Steele, Defoe; men who held the Whig view that the future happiness of England lay not in preserving the traditional economic and social theories and habits of the squirearchy, but in taking full advantage of her great new commercial, industrial, and financial potentialities. Their hero was not Addison's stupid and ridiculous Tory Fox-Hunter (in the *Freeholder*) or Sir Roger de Coverley (an even more effective piece of propaganda than the Fox-Hunter, since it is purportedly a sympathetic portrait, yet it never leaves us in doubt that we may justifiably patronize Sir Roger's essential stupidity), but his and Steele's Sir Andrew Freeport—the name indicates that he believes in abolishing restrictions on trade—

> a merchant of great eminence in the city of London. A person of indefatigable industry, strong reason, and great experience. His notions of trade are noble and generous. . . . [He] will tell you that it is a stupid and barbarous way to extend dominion by arms; for true power is to be got by arts [i.e., technology] and industry. . . . I have heard him prove, that diligence makes more lasting acquisitions than valour. . . . A general trader of good sense is pleasanter company than a general scholar; . . . having a natural unaffected eloquence, the perspicuity of his discourse gives the same pleasure that wit would in another man (*Spectator* No. 2).

Defoe and many others (for instance, Benjamin Franklin in America) wrote innumerable tracts to prove to the general public the truth and importance of Sir Andrew's maxims that "Sloth has ruined more nations than the sword" and that "A penny saved is a penny got." Samuel Johnson might grumble that "Trade could not be managed by those who manage it if it had much difficulty," but Addison reinforced the *Spectator*'s teaching by declaring that

> There is no place in the town which I so much love to frequent as the Royal [stock] Exchange. . . . [It] gratifies my vanity, as I am an Englishman, to see so rich an assembly of countrymen and foreigners, consulting together upon the private business of mankind,

and making this metropolis a kind of emporium for the whole earth. . . . There are not more useful members in a commonwealth than merchants (*Spectator* No. 69).

Pope's and Dryden's denunciations were in vain; the views of Addison and Defoe triumphed. In a canceled line in Pope's tale of Balaam, the successful City merchant, there occurred the simile "rich as P——." This was Thomas Pitt, Governor of Madras, who, by interloping on the preserves of the East India Company, raised himself by sheer nerve and determination from poverty and obscurity to immense wealth. His grandson and great-grandson, the two William Pitts, became in turn the Prime Ministers of the century who most influenced the course of British history, and both owed their success to their alliance with the business community and their ability to inspire the imaginations of the British public with the glories to be obtained by pursuing the course of commercial expansion and international power.

The City of London became more and more powerful as a political force, and in the 1760's Alderman John Wilkes, Alderman Beckford (father of the writer William Beckford), and a host of others took a very active part in the political struggles of the time. On one occasion, at least, Beckford, in the name of the City, insulted George III to his face and was rewarded for his action by the installation of a large plaque in his honor in the Guildhall, the city hall of London. Bristol, too, was thriving, with the expansion of trade with the Americas—especially with the West Indies, where sugar cane plantations (worked by slave labor) were a source of much wealth to English owners. Seeking to impose its will on its Member of Parliament, Burke, it was snubbed by him in a classic speech on the duty of a representative to the welfare of the nation as a whole rather than to the special interests of his constituents. It may be argued, however, that the force of the business interest in Britain has been somewhat mitigated, from the eighteenth century onward, by the compulsion felt by English businessmen, when they have acquired enough money, to buy rural seats and endeavor to remove the stigma of trade by adopting the habits and views of the squirearchy.

The story of how the British flag followed British trade—the story of the creation of the British Empire—will be told in the next chapter. Meanwhile at home the spirit of enterprise flowered in the "industrial revolution"—the relatively sudden series of advances in industrial technology that, along with the accession of new markets and sources of raw material which resulted from the expansion of the overseas empire, was to make Britain the industrial and commercial colossus she became in the nineteenth century.

The spirit of the "projector"—the modern equivalent might be "operator" or even "wheeler-dealer"—had of course been flourishing from the Renaissance onward; even earlier, for the term is a metaphor from the work of the medieval alchemist who seeks some ingenious process to "get rich quick" by turning base metals into gold. It was satirized by Ben Jonson (in *The Alchemist*) and Swift (in Part Three of *Gulliver's Travels*) among others. But even such a conservative as Samuel Johnson was not immune to its charm: early in life he had dealings with Lewis Paul of Birmingham, who had a (sound) design for cotton-spinning machinery, and his exhortation, when his friend Thrale's brewery was being auctioned, perfectly expresses that spirit—"We are not here to sell a parcel of boilers and vats, but the potentiality of growing rich beyond the dreams of avarice."

The industrial revolution included such incidents as James Watt's invention of a practical steam engine as early as the 1760's; cotton- and wool-spinning and weaving machinery by Crompton, Arkwright, and others; improvements in methods of coal mining and iron smelting, and the establishment of new industrial communities in the North near coal beds, the source of power; improved methods of road building, the construction of canals and iron bridges, the establishment of a ceramics industry in Staffordshire by the Wedgwoods. A still greater expansion was to come in the next century, but even in the eighteenth there were such astonishing statistics as an increase in the output of pig iron from 17,000 tons in 1740 to four times that amount in 1788 and eight times it in 1796; in the value of manufactured cotton exported from £14,000 in 1739 to £303,000 in 1779; in the consumption of raw cotton from one million pounds at the beginning of the century to 22 million in 1787.[17]

Britain had, of course, been engaged in industry and commerce before the introduction of steam power. Even in the Middle Ages, she had taken pride in her woolen manufacture—Chaucer's Wife of Bath had "passed hem of Ypres and of Gaunt" in her weaving, and the Lord Chancellor still presides over the House of Lords from the Woolsack, which symbolized its importance. Companies for trading in distant parts of the world were chartered in Elizabeth's day—the East India and the Muscovy Companies—and in Charles II's—the Hudson's Bay Company. When Louis XIV revoked the Edict of Nantes in 1685, withdrawing toleration from French Protestants, many Huguenots came to England and set up a thriving silk-weaving industry in Spitalfields.

Up to the mid-eighteenth century, however, such enterprises had existed along with agriculture in a well balanced and self-contained economy. Now, with Britain's technological superiority over the rest of the world, it seemed reasonable to many (such as Adam Smith and his disciple, the younger Pitt) for her to put all her economic eggs in the one basket of unrestrained commercial and industrial expansion, buying raw materials from the outside, manufacturing them cheaply, and selling the finished product back to the rest of the world at a profit sufficient to enable her to buy food for her population. In the early stages of this transformation Samuel Johnson had warned, with remarkable foresight, of its inherent dangers. "Commerce," he wrote in 1756,

> however we may please ourselves with the contrary opinion, is one of the daughters of fortune, inconstant and deceitful as her mother; she chooses her residence where she is least expected, and shifts her abode, when her continuance is in appearance most firmly settled. . . . It is apparent that every trading nation flourishes . . . by the courtesy of others. We cannot compel any people to buy from us, or to sell to us. A thousand accidents may prejudice them in favour of our rivals; the workmen of another nation may labour for less price, or some accidental improvement, or natural advantage, may procure a just preference to their commodities. . . . Manufactures, indeed, and profitable manufactures, are sometimes raised from imported materials, but then we are subjected a second time to the caprice of our neighbours. The natives of Lombardy might easily resolve to retain their silk at home, and employ workmen of their

own to weave it. And this will certainly be done when they grow wise and industrious, when they have sagacity to discern their true interest, and vigour to pursue it.[18]

Something of this nature did, in fact, happen in the early twentieth century, to the consequent distress of the British economy. But in the excitement of the "potentiality of growing rich beyond the dreams of avarice" which gripped the *entrepreneurs* of the eighteenth century, no one was in a mood to pay much attention to Johnson's gloomy long-term predictions.

The Rest

An attempt has been made above to identify the principal interests in British society of the eighteenth century—the "old money" of the peerage, which was generally Whig; the "new money" of the business community, which was "Pittite"; the agricultural interest of the country gentlemen, who constituted the Tories or Independents. What of the remainder, the vast majority of the population? Here a distinction made by Johnson in his *Dictionary* should be noted: under the word "poor," after listing several of its ordinary meanings, he adds *"The poor* (collectively): Those who are in the lowest rank of the community; those who cannot subsist but by the charity of others; but it is sometimes used with laxity for any not rich." It is the distinction of a shrewd and compassionate observer, who had a good deal of bitter personal knowledge about the importance of that distinction—his father, Michael Johnson, had begun life as one of the poor, since he owed his apprenticeship in his trade of bookseller to the generosity of a charitable organization in Lichfield. Johnson expands on the subject in reviewing the complacent arguments of the well-to-do Soame Jenyns that the poor should be content with their lot:

"Poverty" [writes Johnson] is very gently paraphrased by "want of riches." In that sense almost every man may in his own opinion be poor. But there is another poverty, which is "want of competence," of all that can soften the miseries of life, of all that can diversify attention, or delight imagination. There is yet another poverty, which is "want of necessaries," a species of poverty which no care of the public, no charity of particulars [i.e., individuals], can preserve many from feeling openly, and many secretly.

In affluent eighteenth-century England (as in the affluent twentieth-century United States) there were many of the poor: one statistician placed the number of "paupers . . . vagrants, gipsies, rogues and vagabonds," with incomes of less than £10 per family, in England in 1801 at considerably more than one-eighth of the total population. The same writer's figures give an average family income for the whole population of around £115.[19]

There was no thought, in Johnson's day or for long afterward, of allowing the poor in his sense to share in the government of the nation; it was enough of a task to help them ameliorate their condition and to keep them from starving. (Probably few did: there had been, since Elizabeth's time, an elaborate, if far from wholly satisfactory, system of "poor laws" to relieve them.) Between the poor, however, and those at the other end of the scale, the peerage, the gentry, and the magnates of business, lay the vast majority of the nation—"persons in lesser civil offices, lesser clergymen, lesser freeholders, [tenant] farmers, persons of the law, liberal arts and sciences, artisans, labourers employed in manufactures and building, labouring people in husbandry," to quote some of the categories in the statistical analysis mentioned above.

Writers sometimes speak of the rise of the middle class in the eighteenth century, as though no such class had hitherto existed. But evidently it did (though, to be sure, as time went on it exerted more and more influence in public affairs, the proliferation of newspapers, magazines, and books throughout the century making it more knowledgeable and confident in these matters). Throughout the century there were certainly a great many of what Goldsmith called

the middle order . . . that order of men which subsists between the very rich and the very rabble; those men who are possessed of too large fortunes to submit to the neighboring man of power, and yet are too poor to set up for tyranny themselves. . . . This order is known to be the true preserver of freedom, and may be called *the people* (*The Vicar of Wakefield,* Chap. 19).

It is interesting to find Goldsmith, like his friend Johnson a staunch Tory, thus praising the virtues of the middle order, to which he and Johnson belonged, and, in the passage that follows this, acclaiming the monarch (then George III) as the defender of the rights of that order against the attempted encroachments of the men of power (i.e., the aristocratic Whigs of the Walpole–Newcastle–Rockingham–Fox–Burke tradition). "The time is now come," Johnson begins a number of the *Literary Magazine* at the beginning of the Seven Years' War, "in which *every* Englishman expects to be informed of the national affairs, and in which he has a right to have that expectation gratified"—not merely the men of power.

Indeed, by far the greatest number of the English writers of the eighteenth century belonged to that order which proclaimed its rights in such resounding terms. On the whole, the impression one gets from their writings is of a society more closely resembling that of the United States from the eighteenth century to the present time, in which the bulk of the population, in spite of the diversity of their interests and education and economic status, tend to think of themselves as a fairly homogeneous middle order or "the people." It is at least arguable that the literature of the century gives a picture of a society in which class snobbery was less full grown than it became in nineteenth-century Britain, when the newly affluent business families began to find it necessary to send their children to the many recently founded private schools to acquire the proper "U" accent, still the mark of the middle class, as distinguished from the working class. It is perhaps worth noting that Johnson and Goldsmith, however "zealous for subordination" they may have been, use the terms "rank" and "order" instead of the later "class," which has come to imply a hereditary permanency absent in the other more neutral terms.

In his novel *Peregrine Pickle,* Smollett tells a story—an old one, no doubt—of how, as a joke, his hero picks up a common prostitute, and, after giving her a few *weeks'* training in fashionable jargon and drawing room manners, is able to palm her off as a fine society lady. It is significant that, unlike poor Liza Doolittle in Shaw's version of the story a century and a half later, the girl does not have to endure the *months* of agonizing drill needed to change her vowel patterns from non-U to U ones. That is to say, at least one very formidable barrier to rising in the world was absent.

Indeed, social mobility generally seems to have been easier than it was to become in the next two centuries. Able boys from poor backgrounds frequently rose to the highest rank in the legal, ecclesiastical, and military professions, to distinction in the arts and in business. Johnson himself seemed to move with perfect ease on all social levels, talking with the King or dining with the Duke and Duchess of Argyll with as little embarrassment as with an old schoolfellow, one Jackson, who "had tried to be a cutler at Birmingham, but had not succeeded; and now lived poorly at home and had some scheme of dressing leather in a better manner than common." It is Boswell, who was present and gives the account—Boswell, who so often adumbrates the attitudes of the nineteenth century—who was ill at ease in the encounter with this "low man, dull and untaught," as he calls him, wearing a "coarse great coat, greasy leather breeches, and a yellow uncurled wig," and who marvels at Johnson's "genuine humanity and real kindness" in listening politely to Jackson's "low" conversation.

What did it feel like to be an average citizen of Britain living in the eighteenth century? There has been a good deal of fantasy spun by later writers about "the spirit of the age." Early Romantic writers, rebelling as a younger generation always does against its immediate predecessors, and rejoicing in the freedom of their loose-flowing locks and newly invented trousers, took the wigs, brocades, and tight knee breeches of their grandfathers as symbols of restraint and decorum, and condemned the century as rule-bound, formal, artificial, in contrast to the "naturalness" of their own time. (They forgot that nature decks out the male bird in similarly flamboyant attire for very natural purposes, purposes which history shows the Restoration and eighteenth century, from Charles II on, to have been no more hampered in pursuing than the Romantics were.) After time had diminished the spirit of rebellion, the later nineteenth century no longer condemned the eighteenth century's "artificiality," but rather cherished it, as quaint and amusing, a time of sedan chairs and masquerade balls and bewigged cavaliers and harmless flirtations.

> When dames wore hoops and powdered hair
> And very strict was etiquette,
> When men were brave and ladies fair
> They danced the minuet

were the words someone of Austin Dobson's generation wrote to be sung to the melody of Mozart's minuet in *Don Giovanni*—a piece which, in the opera, takes place in an atmosphere seething with lust, hatred, and violence, with intrigue, murder, and rape.

It was certainly not a placid, secure time for the ordinary citizen. The century began in the midst of a fierce European, indeed "world" war, against the might of Louis XIV; its midpoint was marked by the opening of a still greater one, in which, as Macaulay put it, "black men fought on the coast of Coromandel, and red men scalped each other by the Great Lakes of North America"; it ended in the midst of the greatest of all, that against Napoleon. On the basis of the number of casualties suffered, the American Revolutionary War was merely one of Britain's minor engagements in the century. At home there were the Jacobite rebellions and invasions of 1715, 1718, and 1745, the last a very serious threat indeed, with Scotland lost to the enemy and the rebel army advancing into England as far as the Midlands; and for decades, the problem of Jacobite subversive activity played much the same role in British politics as the Communist threat did in the United States of the 1940's and 1950's. There was frequent rioting and mob violence—over elections, over religious differences, over shortages of food and high prices: the Porteous riots of 1736, the Wilkes riots in the 1760's, and, most violent of all, the Gordon "No Popery" riots of 1780, in which London was in a state of anarchy for a week. Civil order was maintained with the greatest difficulty by the decrepit "watch," figures of fun since the time of Shakespeare's Dogberry; it was not until the Home Secretaryship of Sir Robert Peel in the 1820's that Britain acquired an effective police force. Dorothy George begins the last chapter of her *London Life in the Eighteenth Century* with a summing up: "The dominating impression of life in eighteenth-century London, from the standpoint of the individual, is one of uncertainty and insecurity."

At the same time, it is wrong to react too vigorously to the view of eighteenth-century Britain as a quaint and decorous age of restraint and reason, and to picture it, as some recent historians have, as containing little but crude and callous barbarity. In the opening year of the century, Dryden could look back in disillusionment over the religious and civil strife, the fanaticism and the cynicism that had characterized its predecessor the seventeenth century, and welcome the new era as holding out at least the possibility of something better:

> All, all of a piece throughout:
> Thy chase had a beast in view;
> Thy wars brought nothing about;
> Thy lovers were all untrue.
> 'Tis well an old age is out,
> And time to begin a new.

The promise did not go unfulfilled. The constant threat of civil war and radical political and social upheaval that had plagued England throughout most of Dryden's lifetime at last came to an end when the heirs of the two old warring factions of Cavaliers and Roundheads reached a *modus vivendi* in the wonderfully successful compromise of 1689. It is from this year of the settlement of the Glorious Revolution that "the eighteenth century" perhaps ought to be dated; it is here that one most clearly sees a division in the outlook of those who grew up before and those who grew up after it. In the writings of Dryden and Swift, whose minds were formed in the earlier period, one often detects a nervousness, an underlying insecurity, as if they were never sure when the structure of their society might dissolve beneath their feet, a feeling which is absent in the work of the post-Revolutionary Pope and Johnson, however heartily they may from time to time abuse the contemporary scene.

Savage as the English criminal law was in the eighteenth century, it was less savage than that in France, where the barbarous judicial execution of Robert-François Damien in 1757 raised a horrified protest from the whole of the European intellectual community. It was, after all, the century in which men stopped killing witches, and in which it was judicially decided (by Lord Mansfield in 1772) that slavery could not exist on English soil— nearly a century before a war decided the same thing in the United States.

The increase in the public dissemination of knowledge, in the production and distribution of newspapers, magazines, and books, was phenomenal, and men like Addison and Steele, Johnson and Goldsmith were among the leaders of the movement for enlightened journalism. It was the century when serious writers ceased having to rely on the whims of wealthy patrons in order to be able to pursue their vocation, thanks to such sturdy defenders of the dignity of the creative writer as Pope and Johnson. It was a century with a most distinguished record of sincere and effective charitable and humanitarian activity; and however short it may have fallen of the highest ideal, we of the twentieth century, with its ghastly record of large-scale bloodshed and torture, are hardly in a position to take a supercilious attitude toward the eighteenth in the matter of callousness toward our fellow human beings.

NOTE ON TITLES

A note on British titles of rank, which many students find puzzling, may be helpful. The five ranks of the peerage are, in ascending order, baron, viscount, earl, marquess (the French spelling "marquis" is now seldom used), and duke. Peers of the peerages of England, Great Britain (creations since 1707), and the United Kingdom (creations since 1801) automatically become members of the House of Lords. Members of the peerage of Ireland, before the abolition of the Irish parliament in 1801, were entitled to sit in the Irish House of Lords in Dublin, but not in the British House of Lords; they might, however, be elected to the British House of Commons—Viscount Palmerston, the nineteenth-century Prime Minister, an Irish peer, sat in the Commons as member for an English constituency. The Scottish peers, at the beginning of each new Parliament, elect sixteen of their number to represent them in the British House of Lords—the Earl of Bute, George III's Prime Minister, sat in the Lords as a Scottish representative peer—but the remainder are *not* eligible to the House of Commons. Many Scottish and Irish peers, however, also hold subordinate English (or, after 1707, British) peerages, in right of which they sit in the British House of Lords: e.g., the Earl of Shelburne (peerage of Ireland) sat in the House of Lords as Baron Wycombe (peerage of Great Britain). Baronets (hereditary) and knights (non-hereditary) are not peers, but commoners; they are designated "Sir," with given and family name (as "Sir Robert Walpole"). Wives of peers are, in order, baronesses, viscountesses, countesses, marchionesses, and duchesses. Wives of baronets and knights are "Lady" with the family name only: Maria Skerret, who married Sir Robert Walpole, became "Lady Walpole."

Much confusion is caused by "courtesy titles" and the designations "Lord" and "Lady," none of which are *official* styles of any peer. Eldest surviving sons of earls, marquesses, and dukes are given the "courtesy" title of (usually) the second highest peerage held by the father: e.g., the eldest son of the Duke of Chandos was referred to as the Marquess of Carnarvon (but in official documents merely "Henry Brydges, Esquire, commonly styled Marquess of Carnarvon"). Younger sons of marquesses and dukes bear the courtesy designation "Lord" with given and family names: Lord Sidney Beauclerk, father of Johnson's friend Topham Beauclerk, was fifth son of the Duke of St. Albans. "Lord" with the title only, and without "of," is also the normal designation, except on official occasions, of barons (it would be very unusual to hear a baron addressed as "Baron So-and-so"), and is the informal mode of address of viscounts, earls, and marquesses, but not dukes: e.g., the Marquess of Rockingham was frequently referred to as "Lord Rockingham," but the Duke of Grafton never as "Lord Grafton."

Baronesses (normally) and viscountesses, countesses, and marchionesses (informally) are addressed as "Lady," with the husband's title, but never duchesses. All daughters of earls, marquesses, and dukes are "Lady" with given and family names. When married to a man of lower rank, they change their own family name to their husband's, but retain their own given name: e.g., when Lady Mary Pierrepont, daughter of Evelyn Pierrepont, Duke of Kingston, married Mr. Edward Wortley Montagu, she became Lady Mary Wortley Montagu (her husband remained "Mr. Wortley Montagu"). Marrying a man of higher rank, they assume the title his wife would normally carry: e.g., when Lady Diana Spencer, daughter of Charles Spencer, Duke of Marlborough, married Lord Bolingbroke (2nd Viscount Bolingbroke), she became Viscountess Bolingbroke (Lady Bolingbroke). Divorced from him and married to Topham Beauclerk, she became Lady Diana Beauclerk (Topham remained "Mr. Beauclerk"). The wife of the younger son of a marquess or duke, if of lower rank than her husband, becomes "Lady" with *her husband's* given and family names: Topham Beauclerk's mother was Lady Sidney Beauclerk. Children of peers not entitled to a courtesy "Lord" or "Lady" are "the Honourable" Mr., Miss, or Mrs. So-and-so. But "Right Honourable" is the attribution of members of the King's Privy Council (e.g., the Rt. Hon. Joseph Addison, PC, MP) and of barons, viscounts, and earls (marquesses are "Most Honourable" and dukes "Most Noble"). Dukes, duchesses, and archbishops (but not archbishops' wives) are formally addressed as "Your Grace"; other peers and peeresses and bishops (but not bishops' wives) as "Your Lordship" or "Your Ladyship" (or "My Lord" or "My Lady"). In the Church of England, archbishops are "Most Reverend," bishops "Right Reverend," deans "Very Reverend," and archdeacons "Venerable."

Holders of courtesy titles are not peers but commoners, and may, if elected, sit in the House of Commons: e.g., Lord George Gordon, MP, third son of the Duke of Gordon, and Lord (i.e., Baron—by courtesy)

North, MP, eldest son of the Earl of Guilford ("MP," like "Congressman," indicates a member of the *lower* house of the legislature). However, the heir to a peerage might be summoned (by the Crown) to the House of Lords in one of his father's junior peerages: e.g., John Hervey, second son of the Earl of Bristol, became, on the death of his older brother Carr Hervey in 1723, heir to the earldom; he automatically received the courtesy title Lord (i.e., Baron) Hervey, and was elected to the House of Commons; in 1733, he was given a writ of summons to the House of Lords in his father's peerage of Baron Hervey of Ickworth (i.e., his title was no longer a courtesy but a substantive one, and from a commoner he had become a peer, although his usual designation of "Lord Hervey" remained unchanged).

The title "Lord," with the name of a landed estate, used by Scottish judges has nothing to do with any peerage; it is not hereditary, and it does not confer the epithet "Honourable" on the children of its holders (though Lord Auchinleck's eldest son, James Boswell, used it to impress people on the Continent, who presumably knew no better). Nor does "Lord" in the names of various offices of government (Lord High Chancellor, Lord Keeper of the Privy Seal, Lord Commissioner of the Treasury or Admiralty) have any connection with the peerage, and a Mr. Jones appointed to one of them remains Mr. Jones still.

The numbering of the holders of a peerage begins again each time the title is conferred anew. Thus Aubrey de Vere, 20th and last Earl of Oxford (of the De Vere family) died in 1703; in 1711, Robert Harley was created 1st Earl of Oxford (of the second creation); in the nineteenth century the succession to the earldom died out in the Harley family, and in the 1920's Herbert Henry Asquith was again created 1st Earl of Oxford (of the third creation).

NOTES TO CHAPTER ONE

1. *London Life in the Eighteenth Century* (London: Kegan Paul, 1925; rep. London: London School of Economics, 1951), pp. 36, 42.

2. *History of England* (1849), Chap. I.

3. Maurice Ashley, *The Stuarts in Love* (New York: Macmillan, 1964).

4. It is amusing to find Queen Victoria, born in the last year of her grandfather George III's reign, speaking loftily of "the *bourgeoiserie* of the . . . Russian [imperial] family" (James Pope-Hennessy, *Queen Mary* [New York: Knopf, 1960], pp. 141–142). For all the sneering of the English nobility at them as obscure upstarts, the Hanoverians were fully conscious of their thousand-years descent from Alfred the Great and Guelf the First, and its vast superiority to that of the *parvenu* seventeenth-century Romanovs—and to that of most of the British nobility.

5. The point of view was well expressed in Queen Victoria's objection to a proposal to send the Duke of Clarence, heir presumptive to the throne, and his brother, later King George V, on a tour of the British Empire rather than of Europe: "He & Georgie are charming dear good boys, but very *exclusively* English which you [the Prince of Wales, later

King Edward VII] & your brothers are not, & this is a great misfortune. . . . These Colonies offer no opportunities for the cultivation of art or of any historical interest whatever . . . of Italy, Spain, Austria, Hungary, Russia, Turkey & Holland (very interesting) he knows nothing" (Pope-Hennessy, p. 182).

6. Sir Adolphus Ward (*Cambridge Modern History,* [1902-12] VI, 19) vigorously rebuts the story that Madame Kielmansegge, daughter of his father's mistress, the Countess von Platen, was also George's mistress.

7. "No, no, I'll have mistresses!" "Good Lord, that needn't stop you."

8. Recently two medical researchers, Ida Macalpine and Richard Hunter, have apparently cleared up the old mystery. The few rare attacks of irrationality during George's youth and middle years were the result of the hereditary metabolic disease of porphyria; in old age, he suffered from ordinary arteriosclerotic senility, like Swift. See their *George III and the Mad Business* (London: Allen Lane, 1969).

9. Swift's satire, in *Gulliver's Travels,* of the mutual slaughter of Big-Endians and Little-Endians surely implies Locke's principle, and Johnson frequently affirms it vigorously, e.g., in the preface to his translation of Father Lobo's *Voyage to Abyssinia:* how, he asks, can the Jesuit missionaries to Abyssinia, whose habit was to "preach the gospel with swords in their hands, and propagate by desolation and slaughter the true worship of the God of peace . . . profess themselves the followers of Jesus, who left this great characteristic to his disciples, that they should be known by loving one another, by universal and unbounded charity and benevolence?"

10. An American wit improved on this: "The Puritans thought adultery a greater sin than murder, because adultery gives pleasure to two people but murder only to one."

11. For the student of the Church of England in the eighteenth century, a knowledge of the works of the Very Reverend Norman Sykes, Professor of Ecclesiastical History at Cambridge and later Dean of Winchester, is indispensable. His *Church and State in Eighteenth-Century England* (Cambridge: Cambridge University Press, 1934) and his fine biographies of Archbishop Wake and Bishop Gibson provide a needed corrective to earlier distorted accounts.

12. *History of England,* Chap. III.

13. Because of the rapid fluctuations of the value of money in the twentieth century, it is hard to set a definite equivalent, but a reasonable guess might be that a pound in the eighteenth century was equal in purchasing power to between twenty and forty United States dollars in the 1960's.

14. The premier dukedom of the realm, that of Norfolk, antedated the accession of the Tudor dynasty, but only by two years, having been conferred on John Howard in 1483 by Richard III. On its contemporary holders, Pope commented with his usual pungency,

> What can ennoble sots, or slaves, or cowards?
> Alas! not all the blood of all the Howards.

15. In the 1960's, apparently for the only time in history, the President of the United States and the Prime Minister of Great Britain were re-

lated by marriage, the Prime Minister's wife, Lady Dorothy Macmillan, being aunt to the late Marquess of Hartington, heir to the Dukedom of Devonshire, who had married a sister of President Kennedy. It was thought piquant that the Prime Minister and the President, both grandsons of poor boys who had risen from the Celtic peasantry to great wealth, should be connected through the "ancient" noble house of Cavendish. Yet the Cavendishes had got their start in the reign of Henry VIII by means of the same shrewdness and enterprise that had characterized the careers of Daniel Macmillan and Joseph Kennedy.

16. Students should acquaint themselves with the battle over "wit" that took place around the turn of the century. It was set off by the Reverend Jeremy Collier's blast against contemporary drama, *A Short View of the Immorality and Profaneness of the English Stage* (1698). Since that drama was distinguished for its "wit," wit was thus charged with being the handmaid of immorality (as probably many people still believe, consciously or unconsciously). Collier was supported by the Whig physician and writer of ponderous epics, Sir Richard Blackmore. Congreve replied in defense of wit, but the anti-wit faction carried the day, in drama at least. There were certainly important political implications in the contest, Whiggism and Nonconformity generally championing "morality" as against wit; and when, after the accession of George I, Steele was rewarded for his services as Whig propagandist by being given the patent to operate the Theatre Royal, Drury Lane, he dropped witty Congrevian drama in favor of his own "sentimental comedy," the ancestor of modern soap-opera. If some events in the history of eighteenth-century taste have been termed "pre-Romantic," this episode may be said to illustrate "pre-Victorianism," the spirit that impelled the Reverend Charles Kingsley to exhort, "Be good, sweet maid, and let who will be clever." However, numerous eighteenth-century writers, from Pope, Swift, and Johnson down to Jane Austen, still adhered to the old-fashioned view that being clever might help one to be good. For further discussion, see William Empson, "Wit in the *Essay on Criticism*," *Hudson Review* (Winter 1950) 559–577 (reprinted in his *The Structure of Complex Words* [New York: New Directions, 1951]), and E. N. Hooker, "Pope on Wit: the *Essay on Criticism*," in R. F. Jones *et al.*, *The Seventeenth Century* (Stanford: Stanford University Press, 1951), pp. 604–617.

17. H. Heaton, "Industry and Trade," in A. C. Turberville, ed., *Johnson's England* (Oxford: The Clarendon Press, 1933), I, pp. 231, 239.

18. "Further Thoughts on Agriculture," *Universal Visiter* (March 1756).

19. P. Colquhon, quoted by Dorothy George, *England in Transition* (Penguin Books, 1953), pp. 152–153.

Two

A
Historical
Summary: *1660–1789*

From the Restoration to the
"Glorious Revolution": 1660–1688

Chronology: 1658–1689

1658   Cromwell dies. For a short time his son Richard rules as Protector, but serious divisions occur in the Army leadership. General Monk allows the remnant of the Long Parliament to reconvene; it offers the throne to the exiled Charles II.

1660   Charles II returns, and the "old constitution" is restored. Punitive action is taken against the "regicides" and a few other parliamentary leaders, but an Act of Grace pardons all others. Restrictive laws against Puritanism in religion are passed by the new royalist Parliament (the Clarendon Code, after Charles' chief minister, the Earl of Clarendon). As a result, two thousand Puritan ministers leave the Church of England, becoming Dissenters (Nonconformists). The Royal Society (of London for Improving Natural Knowledge) is founded.

1665   An epidemic of bubonic plague devastates London (see Defoe, *A Journal of the Plague Year*).

1666   The Great Fire of London. The heart of the City is reduced to rubble, including the old Gothic St. Paul's Cathedral. Sir Christopher Wren is commissioned to redesign the City, and later builds a new St. Paul's, in Renaissance–baroque style.

1667   War with Holland, in which the Dutch ravage the English seacoast (see the opening of Dryden's *An Essay of Dramatic Poesy*). Clarendon dismissed and exiled; succeeded by the Cabal, a group of five politicians who seek an alliance with Louis XIV of France. In the secret Treaty of Dover (1670),

Charles accepts Louis' financial aid to enable Charles eventually to restore Roman Catholicism in England.

1668 Sir William Temple (afterward Swift's patron) negotiates the Triple Alliance of England, Holland, and Sweden, a Protestant alliance to curb the growing power of Louis XIV.

1672 William of Orange, the young Stadholder of Holland (next heir to the British throne after James, Duke of York, and his daughters), sets himself up as Louis' chief opponent and leader of Protestantism in Europe. He marries (1677) Princess Mary, eldest daughter of James.

1678 The "Popish Plot"—the informer Titus Oates produces forged "proofs" of a plot of the Catholics to overthrow the government, murder Charles, and place James (a Catholic) on the throne. The agitation is fanned by extreme Protestants led by the Earl of Shaftesbury.

1679– Shaftesbury introduces the Exclusion Bill in Parliament, ex-
81   cluding James from succession to the throne. It is defeated after Charles dissolves Parliament and summons a new one in the more royalist atmosphere of Oxford. Eventually Shaftesbury dies and the agitation simmers down, followed by severe reprisals on his followers.

1685 Charles II dies. James succeeds as King James II. The Duke of Monmouth, Charles' oldest illegitimate son, one of the extreme Protestant faction, invades England (from Holland) and tries to seize power. He is easily defeated and is executed. His followers are ruthlessly punished by Jeffreys, James' Lord Chief Justice, at the "Bloody Assizes."

1685– James initiates a campaign to increase the authority of the
88   Crown and to revive Roman Catholicism in England, by use of the royal prerogative of "suspension"—blanket pardons for offenders against anti-Catholic Acts of Parliament—and "declarations of indulgence" of nonconformity with the Church of England. In 1688, the Archbishop of Canterbury (William Sancroft) and six other bishops present to James a petition protesting against his policy; they are imprisoned in the Tower of London on a charge of sedition. The courts triumphantly acquit them. A son (later, the Old Pretender) is born to James' second wife, making the Protestant princesses Mary and Anne no longer heirs to the throne. Great public agitation.

1688 William of Orange is invited by a number of English leaders to come to England with a Dutch army and restore the rights threatened by James. He does so, and wins widespread support. James flees to France with his wife and young son (the "Glorious Revolution").

1689   William and Mary are proclaimed King and Queen by Parliament and accept the Bill of Rights, which asserts, in effect, the supremacy of Parliament over the King. An act requiring office holders to swear to their belief in the right of the new sovereigns to the throne results in a number of Anglican clergymen giving up their appointments in the Church (the "non-jurors"); also in the retirement of Dryden as Poet Laureate. The Act of Toleration practically guarantees freedom of worship to Protestants outside the Church of England. William forms the Grand Alliance with Spain and Austria, and begins war against Louis XIV (the War of the League of Augsburg).

The Search for Political Stability

There have been few periods when the literature of the time has been more politically conscious than that of the Restoration and the eighteenth century in Britain; perhaps the only parallel that comes readily to the mind is that of America in the 1930's. Dryden, Marvell, Pope, Swift, Addison, Steele, Johnson, Goldsmith, Burke, to mention only some of the greater figures writing between 1660 and 1785, were intensely aware of the political issues of their time, deeply committed to one side or the other, and intent on making their readers understand their significance. Dryden, Swift, Addison, Steele and Johnson all acted as quasi-official publicists for the administrations of their day. Dryden and Swift, indeed, at times, were almost Ministers of Propaganda for their governments, as, earlier, Milton had been for his. For the modern reader fully to understand their writings, he needs at least as good a knowledge of the salient historical events of the reigns of the later Stuart and earlier Hanoverian monarchs as he does of the administrations of Herbert Hoover and Franklin D. Roosevelt in order to understand Steinbeck and Dos Passos (or, for that matter, of fifth-century Athens to understand Aristophanes).

But the student needs to use great caution when reading the older standard political histories of seventeenth- and eighteenth-century Britain—those of Macaulay, J. R. Green, Lecky, and G. M. Trevelyan, among others. The nineteenth-century historians imposed on the facts of the political structure of Britain during this period their own "Whig interpretation," as it has been called. This is probably an unfortunate term. It is true that the interpretation was largely the work of those staunch Whigs, Burke and Macaulay, who certainly used it in the service of their party's welfare. But what is objectionable about it is not that it tends to present Whigs as the heroes and Tories as the villains of eighteenth-century political history—a history may be frankly biased yet useful—but that it grossly oversimplifies and distorts the highly complex terms of political life of the time, reducing them to a dichotomy between forward-looking Whigs and backward-looking Tories. (And, by regarding forward-looking as necessarily good and backward-looking as bad, implicitly postulating the Victorian state of things as the ideal— "ratifying the present," as the inventor of the term "the Whig interpretation," Herbert Butterfield, put it.)

In fact, far from there being a simple two-party system such as developed in mid-nineteenth-century Britain, there were hardly parties at all in the modern sense. There were fluctuating groups of politicians allied for shorter or longer periods of time to promote common interests, or to aid one another to get and retain power. Sometimes, to be sure, these political groupings were based on definite public issues—one notable instance, in the period between 1708 and 1713, was the question of whether the war with France should be continued or whether peace should be made.

But usually the British political structure of the eighteenth century is better understood by thinking of it in terms of modern American politics. There the application of the labels "Republican" and "Democrat" is very often only the result of historical accident and guarantees very little about the ideology of their possessors, where one group of Republicans and one of Democrats may be far closer to each other on most issues than either is to another wing of the same party, where a Democratic Chief Executive may rely on the advice of Republicans whom he has appointed to his Cabinet and find his strongest opposition in a group of Democratic congressmen. It may be wrong to suggest, as Sir Lewis Namier (who demonstrated the falsity of the nine-teenth-century historians' picture) and some of his followers have perhaps done, that eighteenth-century British political history should be analyzed solely in terms of the personal interests and loyalties of the individuals involved in it, ignoring questions of ideology completely. Nevertheless, it is certainly true that during a great deal of the period—as in other times and places—personalities and power-seeking played a much greater role in political maneuvering than did disinterested adherence to abstract principle.

T. S. Eliot once commented that the Civil War in Britain has never ended—that is to say, the basic differences of opinion in politics and religion which divided the country into two war-ring camps in the 1640's still persist today. It is at least true that they were not healed by the Restoration. The return of Charles II from exile in France in 1660, and the replacement of the various short-lived experiments in governmental and ecclesiastical organization under the Parliamentary and Cromwellian regimes by the "old constitution in Church and State"—the resumption of the legislative power by the King-in-Parliament and of the executive power by the King-in-Council, the restoration of the episcopal organization of the Church—were hailed with delight by the vast majority of the English. Pepys' diary gives a striking account of the general rejoicing, and Butler's *Hudibras* is the classic expression of the detestation aroused by the tyrannical dogmatism of the extreme Puritans.

But the sources of discontent which had given rise to the Civil War were by no means eliminated, and again produced bitter strife in 1678, in 1685, and finally in 1688. The political history of the years from 1660 to 1688 is better read as an appendage to that from 1603 to 1660 than as a prelude to that from 1689 onward, and the custom in literary histories of making the seventeenth century terminate and the eighteenth century commence in 1660 seems less and less justifiable the more closely one studies both the history and the literature of the reigns of Charles II and James II. The life of the greatest literary figure of the time, Dryden, overlapped that of Milton by forty-three years, and that of Pope by only twelve; it really makes much more sense to study Dryden and Milton together, as inhabitants of almost the same historical milieu, than it does to lump Dryden together with Pope.

The Restoration of 1660 began as a compromise among the two opposing factions; it was arranged by the Parliamentarian General Monk on the understanding that there would be no reprisals against the Puritan and Parliamentarian side and, for a time at least, this agreement was adhered to. By comparison with the termination of some twentieth-century conflicts, it was a remarkably mild settlement: an Act of Grace initiated by the King guaranteed immunity from prosecution for war crimes to everyone except those who had passed sentence of death on Charles I (the "regicides"), and only a handful of these actually suffered. Even the great propagandist of the regime, John Milton, escaped with no more than a short period of house arrest—a far different fate from that of, for example, Goebbels in the twentieth century. To the Puritan ministers of the Church of England, there was promised a conference to see whether differences could be reconciled, and bishoprics in the Church were offered to two of the Puritan leaders, Baxter and Calamy, though they declined the honor.

Unfortunately, this era of good feeling did not survive the election of the first House of Commons under Charles II, in 1661, the so-called Cavalier Parliament, filled with representatives of the old squirearchy burning for vengeance on those who had confiscated their property and killed their relations in battle (the parallel with what happened in the American South two centuries later is obvious). Its members pushed Charles and his ministers much further than Charles, a most tolerant person even though his tolerance may have stemmed from general political and religious indifference, would himself have gone. Unable, because of the Act of Grace, to inflict civil punishment on their old enemies, they concentrated on ecclesiastical matters, and, with the encouragement of Charles' chief minister, the old Earl of Clarendon, a relic of the days of Charles I and the exile in France, passed a series of stringent statutes (the Clarendon Code) against those in the Church with Puritan leanings.

As a result, some two thousand clergy were forced to leave the Church of England and be classed as "Dissenters" or "Noncon-

formists." The Conventicle Act, the Five-Mile Act, the Corporation Act severely restricted the civil rights and freedom of worship of those who did not adhere to the state church. The Test
Act, passed somewhat later (1672), required all officers of the
state, civil and military, to prove their orthodoxy by taking
communion according to the form of the Church of England
(and produce a certificate to the effect that they had done so),
and to sign a declaration repudiating belief in the doctrine of
transubstantiation. This latter provision was directed at Roman
Catholics rather than Protestant Dissenters, who of course had
no objection to signing such a declaration. Protestant Dissenters,
too, were often willing to receive communion in the Anglican
form at stated times in order to hold a municipal office. An
attempt was made in the reign of Anne to suppress this practice
of "occasional conformity," but without much effect. In fact,
these acts did not really hamper the Nonconformists from prac-
ticing their religion or taking active part in public life, but they
were minor irritations that did not conduce to civil harmony.

It is not necessary here to follow in detail the tortuous political intrigues of the first two decades of Charles' reign, in which
the venerable Clarendon was ousted from power and exiled, and
succeeded first by the Cabal—Clifford, Ashley (later the Earl of
Shaftesbury), Buckingham, Arlington, Lauderdale—and then
by Thomas Osborne, Earl of Danby. In foreign policy, Charles
wavered between friendship with Catholic France under the aggressive Louis XIV, and with Protestant Holland under its
young Stadholder, William of Orange. In the former phase, in
return for a subsidy from France, he agreed by the secret Treaty
of Dover to assist France to crush Holland and (eventually) to
proclaim his own conversion to Roman Catholicism, in the hope
that that of the whole country would follow (it was, however,
kept secret until after his death). In the latter phase, he agreed
to the Triple Alliance of England with Protestant Holland and
Sweden to check the power of Louis, and to the marriage of his
elder niece, Mary, eventual heiress presumptive to the throne,
with William. Mary and her sister Anne, daughters of James,
Duke of York, by his first wife, Anne Hyde, Clarendon's daughter, had been, by Charles' order, educated as Protestants, in
spite of their father's intransigent Catholicism and Charles' own
waverings in that direction.

The question of the future religion of the monarch was to provide a focus for the animosities of the two opposing interests that continued to survive in English political life from the time of the Civil War and earlier. Charles' wife, Catherine of Bragança (of the Portuguese royal family), was sterile, and the immediate heir to the throne was his brother James, who made no secret of his fervent devotion to Rome. Fear of James' succession, however, was mitigated for a time by the assumption that he, in turn, would be succeeded by his staunchly Protestant daughters.

But in the late 1670's, the unscrupulous Anthony Ashley Cooper, first Earl of Shaftesbury (Dryden's Achitophel), found himself out of office and determined to use any means to recover political power. He prevailed on the weak-minded Duke of Monmouth (Absalom), Charles' oldest illegitimate son, to allow himself to be set up as a competitor to James, and, to the accompaniment of a country-wide campaign of anti-Catholic propaganda, introduced into Parliament the Exclusion Bill, which would bar James from succeeding to the throne. All the old antagonisms of the Civil War revived; it was at this time that the terms "Whigs" (to designate supporters of the bill) and "Tories" (to designate its opponents) began to be used—though the student would be wrong to think that these words, at this or any other time in the seventeenth and eighteenth centuries, stood for the tightly organized parties that "Liberal" and "Conservative" came to signify in later nineteenth-century Britain.

At the same time, the rascally Titus Oates "discovered" the great "Popish Plot," in which the Catholics were said to have planned to assassinate Charles and other political leaders and place James on the throne. With Shaftesbury feeding the flames, a small reign of terror against Catholics ensued—some thirty-five individuals were executed for treason. It seriously looked as though the Civil War were about to break out all over again. But Charles, displaying a genius for political maneuver he seldom bothered to exercise—and assisted by his Poet Laureate Dryden's great *Absalom and Achitophel* ("Of this poem," wrote Johnson, "the reception was eager, and the sale so large, that my father, an old bookseller, told me he had not known it equalled but by Sacheverell's Trial," thirty years later)—managed in time, by judicious alternations of compliance and firmness, to quiet the disturbance; Shaftesbury was forced to flee into exile, and at Charles' death in 1685, James peacefully ascended the throne.

He occupied it for only three hectic years, during which his incredible ineptness managed to alienate all factions of his subjects, Whig and Tory, Anglican and Nonconformist. A rebellion raised in the West by Monmouth was crushed and its participants punished (in the "Bloody Assizes" conducted by James' sadistic Lord Chief Justice Jeffreys) with a ferocity which appalled even the great numbers of his subjects who sympathized with James as against Monmouth. The climax came late in 1688, when he sent seven bishops of the Church of which he was officially head, including the Archbishop of Canterbury, to the Tower on charges of sedition, and when his second wife unexpectedly gave birth to a son, who automatically displaced the Protestant Mary and Anne from the succession to the throne and who would assuredly be brought up as a Catholic. This was too much to be borne. An invitation was quickly sent to William of Orange to come over with an army and restore the *status quo*. He did so. James' supporters—including his daughter Anne —flocked to William's banner, and James fled to France without offering any opposition. William and Mary were proclaimed King and Queen, and the Glorious—and bloodless—Revolution was accomplished.

It is hard to resist using the jocular cliché that James II was a "bad King" but a "good thing." No one could have succeeded better in demonstrating to the opposing groups of Englishmen how much they had in common which it was to their interest to preserve. Tories and Whigs, Royalists and Parliamentarians alike were threatened with an absolutism foreign to the English tradition; Anglicans and Nonconformists alike were threatened with domination by Rome. The Revolution of 1688, as has often been pointed out (especially by Burke, contrasting it with the violence and dogmatism of the French Revolution), was an intense expression of *conservatism*. The banner of William's invading army bore the motto of the House of Orange, "Je maintiendrai" ("I will maintain"). What was confirmed by the expulsion of James and by the Declaration of Rights drawn up by the Parliamentary Convention which offered the throne to William and Mary (who signed that Declaration) was the ancient English tradition of limited monarchy and government by consent. The legislative power was to remain in the hands of the King-in-Parliament, and was not to be subverted by suspensions of Acts of Parliament by the king alone, such as James had practiced. Parliament was to have the power to determine the succession to the throne, a power confirmed by the act of William and Mary in accepting their crowns from the hands of Parliament, and a little later, by the Act of Settlement, 1701, which passed over several dozen persons with a better hereditary claim (including James II's son, the Old Pretender) to settle the crown on the Protestant Electors of Hanover. (This was nothing new in English history—the Lancastrian dynasty of Henry IV and the Tudor of Henry VII had been placed on the throne, with Parliamentary consent, to the exclusion of closer heirs.)

Judged on the basis of its results in England, the Revolution of 1688 was enormously successful. There were a few dissentients: some Roman Catholics (but not all—Pope Innocent XI by no means approved of the activities of the Jesuits who guided James' counsels, and refused to make the chief of them, Father Petre, a cardinal when James asked him to do so); some Anglicans (the "non-jurors"), including Archbishop Sancroft of Canterbury, who, maintaining that only James had the hereditary, and therefore divine, right to the throne, refused to take the required oaths recognizing William and Mary as the lawful sovereigns, and were deprived of their appointments (Dryden lost his post of Poet Laureate in this way). But to the vast majority, it was the inevitable solution of an intolerable situation. Tories claimed as much credit for it as Whigs; in later years even "High Tories" such as Swift and Johnson expressed their approval of it. It was the last time that there has been a serious attempt to change the basic terms of government in England by internal force (this is not true, of course, of Scotland and Ireland). A general agreement had at last been reached on what those terms were to be, and, although the old animosities of the seventeenth century were not yet completely healed, it was recognized that a broad enough framework of political agreement existed that minor differences within that framework could be tolerated.

This was finally proven when Harley, Earl of Oxford, fell from power on the change of dynasty in 1714. In the previous century, when such a leader was ousted by his enemies, severe reprisals at once overtook him: Strafford was executed, Clarendon was exiled. For two years Oxford was kept imprisoned and threatened with impeachment on a charge of treason. But the impeachment was at last dropped—thanks to Robert Walpole's maneuverings behind the scenes—and Oxford was released. Even more strikingly, when Walpole in turn fell from power in 1742—and few politicians have made more virulent enemies than Walpole did during his long term of office—although a strenuous effort was made to have him impeached, it too quickly failed; Oxford's son was one of many Tories who refused to vote against Walpole. Since that time the right to the existence of a "loyal opposition" has been recognized, and England—along with other countries, such as the United States, which have inherited the English tradition of government—has been spared the turmoil and bloodshed which in other places has accompanied a shift in political power. The principle of political as well as religious toleration was able to subsist because of the establishment by the Revolution of basic terms of government on which the vast majority of the English could agree. The political stability thus attained has seen England safely through two and a half centuries of internal peace, and certainly accounts for a good deal of the release of national energy which characterized the England of the eighteenth century.

From the Revolution to the Peace of Paris: 1688–1769

Chronology: 1690–1763

1690   Military campaigns against James' supporters in Scotland and Ireland. William defeats James at the Battle of the Boyne (July 12, N.S.) and subdues Ireland.

1694   Queen Mary dies of smallpox. Bank of England founded—modern conception of state financing, with a permanent national debt.

1697 War with France ended by the inconclusive Treaty of Ryswick.

1701 War with France (War of the Spanish Succession) again touched off by an attempt of Louis XIV to place his grandson on the vacant throne of Spain. James II dies in exile in France, bequeathing his claim to the British throne to his son, James Edward (their supporters known as "Jacobites," from Latin *Jacobus*, James). The Act of Settlement provides that after the death of Anne (who has no living children) the Crown go to Sophia, Electress of Hanover in Germany, the nearest Protestant heir, and that the sovereign and his consort must be Protestants (the act is still in force).

1702 William III dies from a fall from his horse. Succeeded by Anne (her husband, Prince George of Denmark, a nonentity, dies 1708). John Churchill, Duke of Marlborough, appointed commander of English and allied forces in the war against France; his wife, Sarah, dominates Anne.

1704 Marlborough decisively defeats the French at the Battle of Blenheim. Whigs, with the Earl of Godolphin as Lord Treasurer (prime minister), control the government and vigorously prosecute the war with France.

1707 Act of Union between England and Scotland. Scotland's separate parliament is abolished and Scots send representatives to the Parliament at London. Official name of the nation becomes "Great Britain" (the geographical name of the island, distinguished from "Little Britain"—Brittany in France).

1709 The Whig administration prosecutes Henry Sacheverell, a Tory High Churchman, for a sermon deploring the Revolution. Sacheverell becomes regarded as a martyr, and the Whigs lose popularity. The Duchess of Marlborough quarrels with Anne and is eventually dismissed, replaced by the Tory Lady Masham as the Queen's confidante.

1710 Whigs dismissed from government, replaced by the Tories Robert Harley, Earl of Oxford, and Henry St. John, Viscount Bolingbroke, with Swift as their chief publicist. Negotiations begun to end the war with France, which the Tories feel is being unnecessarily prolonged for the benefit of Marlborough and the Whigs. Stricter measures against Nonconformists urged by High Church Tories.

1713 War with France ended by Tory-negotiated Peace of Utrecht (chief negotiator, the poet Matthew Prior).

1714   Harley and St. John quarrel. Anne dies; a Whig council of
regency (secretary, Joseph Addison) takes over power while
awaiting arrival of the new king George I, Elector of Hanover
(his mother, Electress Sophia, having died a short time before
Anne). On George's arrival, all Tories are dismissed, and the
first of a series of Whig administrations takes over, lasting
until the end of the century. Bolingbroke, accused of treason-
able plotting to restore the throne to the Pretender, flees to
France, and joins the Pretender. Oxford is impeached and
imprisoned, but eventually released.

1715   Invasion of Scotland by forces headed by the Old Pretender
("the '15"). It is quickly crushed, and the leaders executed.
James Edward escapes back to France.

1721   The South Sea Bubble—a vast speculative scheme for trading
in the Pacific—collapses and causes financial chaos. Several
leading members of the Whig government are implicated and
discredited; Robert Walpole, leader of an opposition Whig
faction, becomes prime minister (for twenty years).

1727   George I dies; succeeded by his son George II (with whom he
has quarreled constantly) and the intellectual and skeptical
Queen Caroline.

1733   Opposition to Walpole increased by his attempt to impose
a heavy Excise Act (he is forced to withdraw it). The opposition consists largely of Whigs alienated by Walpole ("the
Patriots"), led by William Pulteney and Lord Carteret, later
joined by William Pitt (the elder), representing the formidable commercial interests which feel Walpole is unnecessarily
cautious in promoting Britain's development into a world-
wide trading nation. Bolingbroke, permitted to return from
exile, and Frederick, Prince of Wales, George II's foolish son
and heir, support the opposition against Walpole.

1738   Agitation by the opposition for war with Spain, which has
vigorously resisted infringement by British merchants of her
monopoly of trading in South American and Pacific waters
(guaranteed by the Peace of Utrecht). Captain Jenkins exhi-
bits to a Parliamentary investigating committee an ear
allegedly cut off by a Spanish coastguard captain.

1739   Walpole reluctantly declares war against Spain, prosecutes it
half-heartedly and unsuccessfully.

1741–   Walpole loses support in a general election, and is finally
42   forced to resign; becomes Earl of Orford. Succeeded by a
Whig coalition of former allies and opponents of Walpole,

in which Henry Pelham and his brother, the Duke of New-castle, eventually attain leadership. The Spanish war develops into the War of the Austrian Succession, started by Frederick (the Great) of Prussia's aggression against the territories of Maria Theresa of Austria.

1743   George II personally leads an English and Hanoverian army to victory over the French at the Battle of Dettingen.

1745   Invasion of Scotland by Charles Edward, the Young Pre-tender. The Jacobite forces penetrate as far south as central England. But expected English support is not forthcoming, and Charles retreats to Scotland. His forces are eventually routed at the Battle of Culloden by the Duke of Cumberland, George II's younger son. Charles escapes to France. One result of "the '45" is the beginning of an attempt to civilize the Highlands of Scotland and abolish the remains of the feudal clan system.

1748   The shaky Peace of Aix-la-Chapelle with France is concluded.

1750's and 1760's. Development of new machinery—James Watt's steam engine, wool- and cotton-spinning and weaving ma-chinery—which is to revolutionize industry in Britain: the beginning of the Industrial Revolution.

1751   Frederick, Prince of Wales, dies; succeeded as heir to the throne by his twelve-year-old son George. His tutor, the Earl of Bute, one of Frederick's political associates (a Scot), brings up George in the "Patriot" and oppositionist tradition of Frederick.

1751–   Continued clashes between neighboring French and British
56   settlements in North America and India, where the French also pursue an expansionist policy. French troops move southward in the Ohio valley, cutting off the British colonies of the Atlantic seaboard from expansion to the west; they seize Fort Duquesne (now Pittsburgh); an expedition to retake it, led by General Braddock, is disastrously defeated.

1756   War between France, on one side, and Britain and Prussia on the other, is declared (the Seven Years' War). William Pitt, a dissident Whig leader, reconciles his differences with the official Whig leadership under Newcastle, and becomes virtual prime minister, conducting the war with great vigor and success. Wolfe later defeats the French in Canada and Clive in India.

1760   George II dies (aged 77); succeeded by his grandson George III (aged 22). The older Whig factions led by Newcastle and

Pitt are in disfavor; Bute becomes Prime Minister, and pursues a policy of bringing the war to a close.

1763   Peace of Paris; Canada and India are ceded to Britain.

The Rise of Greater Britain

William III's twelve-year reign was largely occupied in consolidating the Revolution—Jacobite uprisings in Scotland were crushed, and Ireland, where James himself proceeded with a French army, needed over two years of hard fighting to subdue; mediating among squabbling factions of his English political advisers; and conducting a Continental war against France (the War of the League of Augsburg, concluded by the shaky Treaty of Ryswick, 1697). Two domestic events were of particular significance. The chartering of the Bank of England, conceived by the brilliant financier (and dilettante poet and patron of the arts, possibly a model for Pope's Bufo) Charles Montagu, later Earl of Halifax, provided for the first time a modern scheme of national financing. This included the indispensable national debt, which enabled Britain to engage in long-term military operations and acted as the nucleus for a system of commercial banking on which more ambitious commercial and industrial enterprises could be based. The failure of Parliament to renew or replace the act requiring printed materials to be inspected and licensed before publication put an end to the centuries-old principle of prepublication censorship, and the beginning of an era of freedom of the press; though once published, books and periodicals were subject to the laws of libel and sedition, as of course they still are. (Strangely, censorship, after being removed from the press, was imposed, in 1737, on the London stage, Walpole having lost his patience with the scathing lampoons on him that were being presented. Until 1968, a play to be performed publicly in London had to be approved in advance by the Lord Chamberlain's office.)

William's cold efficiency and his preference for Holland and his Dutch advisers made him few friends in England, and his early death, when his horse tripped over a mole hill, was not much lamented in his adopted country. Indeed, Holland became in the Tories' eyes the symbol of all they did not wish

England to be: it was accused of crass commercialism and materialism, of being a country where wealth was the highest value and the rich were at liberty to exploit the poor as they pleased. Yet even Johnson and Swift, who printed as much anti-Dutch propaganda as anyone—one of Swift's most notable contributions was the conclusion of Book Three of *Gulliver's Travels* where the Dutch are ascribed the pleasant habit of trampling on the crucifix to please the Japanese with whom they want to trade—admit, with varying degrees of reluctance, that the replacement of James II with William III was necessary.

James died in France in 1701, shortly before his nephew and son-in-law, William; and Louis XIV comforted James on his deathbed, and helped to set Europe in flames again, by recognizing his son James Edward as King James III of England. Most of the reign of Anne, William's successor, was occupied with the War of the Spanish Succession, which Louis' action, among other things, helped to ignite. The main question at issue was whether the succession to the Spanish throne should or should not go to Louis' grandson, who was one of the closest in the hereditary succession. The deeper question was whether French power should be allowed to expand by the addition of the power of Spain and her far-flung colonies, so as to dominate the competition that was developing for world trade and empire among the European powers. The English Whigs were determined that it should not, and John Churchill, Duke of Marlborough, husband of Anne's favorite, Sarah, and a brilliant general and diplomat, was resolved to implement that determination. By a series of great victories on the Continent—Blenheim, Ramilies, Oudenarde, Malplaquet—he crushed French military might, but at enormous expense in bloodshed. The number of casualties in these battles of Marlborough surpassed anything Britain had hitherto known; in its scope and ferocity, the War of the Spanish Succession might be termed the first of the modern world wars. This casualty rate accounts for at least some of the animosity Swift and other Tories displayed against Marlborough, for instance, in Swift's bitter "epitaph" on him:

> Behold his funeral appears,
> Nor widows' sighs, nor orphans' tears,

> Wont at such times each heart to pierce,
> Attend the progress of his hearse.
> But what of that? his friends may say,
> He had those honours in his day.
> True to his profit and his pride,
> He made them weep before he died.

Toward 1708 the great issue in English domestic politics became that of the continuation of the war. The Whigs and Marlborough, with their publicists Steele and Addison, insisted that to terminate it before France was eliminated as an important military power was short-sighted. If she were allowed to retain any substantial strength, they maintained, her aggression would eventually have to be checked all over again. Moreover, for Britain to withdraw unilaterally would be a betrayal of her Continental allies. The Tories argued, to the contrary, that Britain's aims in the war had been achieved, that France had learned her lesson, and that Marlborough, the Whigs, and the allies wished to continue the war merely for reasons of aggrandizement and personal advantage. The Tories got their way. In 1710, with the help of the Duchess of Marlborough, whose haughty temper finally overcame Anne's devotion to her, the Whig ministers were dismissed, and the famous Tory ministry of Harley, Earl of Oxford, and St. John, Viscount Bolingbroke, with Swift as their chief propagandist, came into power. The Peace of Utrecht, negotiated largely by the poet Matthew Prior, who was in the diplomatic service, was concluded in 1713.

The hectic political activity of the last years of Anne's reign, when Harley and Bolingbroke engaged in an internecine contest for sole power and both were alarmed by the probability that after Anne's death their Whig opponents, with the support of the new King, would take office, is brilliantly reported in Swift's *Journal to Stella* and (in fictional form) in Thackeray's *Henry Esmond*. There is no real evidence for the suggestion of Thackeray and others that the Tory leaders were plotting to give the crown to James III instead of to George I; yet all of them, including some Whig leaders, kept in some kind of touch with the Jacobite headquarters on the Continent—just in case. The presence of the Jacobite threat during the early decades of the eighteenth century—until after its last desperate attempt in the

Scottish rebellion of 1745—was closely analogous in the political history of the time to the Communist threat in the Western countries in the 1940's and 1950's. Jacobite espionage and subversive activity certainly did go on; at the same time, astute Whigs made political capital for themselves by exaggerating it and freely accusing their opponents of "Jacobite tendencies" when it suited their book to do so. Conversely, thoughtful Tories like Samuel Johnson risked the charge of Jacobitism by condemning these tactics by the Whigs. There is no evidence whatever that Johnson was a Jacobite, in the sense of seriously wishing the restoration of the Stuart family to the throne; but he was certainly an "anti-anti-Jacobite," to adapt a modern phrase.

How little real hold Jacobitism had on the English was demonstrated in "the '45" when the army of Prince Charles Edward (the Young Pretender), managing to advance as far south into England as Derby, found the lip service of the English Jacobites to be no more than that. No crowds of English reinforcements flocked to Charles's banner and he was forced to retreat to Scotland, where English military might soon overpowered him at the Battle of Culloden.[1] The last Stuart claimant to the throne, Charles' younger brother Henry, "Duke of York" and Cardinal of the Roman Catholic Church ("King Henry IX" according to the Jacobites), died in 1807, recipient of a pension from his distant cousin George III to help relieve his necessities.

With the constitutional question settled by the Revolution of 1688, and the problem of French aggression solved, for the time being at least, by the Peace of Utrecht, the energies of English politicians were free to be applied to the great central contest in the history of the first half of the eighteenth century. Britain had to choose whether she was to remain a self-contained, isolationist nation, avoiding foreign and imperial entanglements (a "little England," to use the term that was coined when the question was again debated in the middle of the nineteenth century), or whether she was to take advantage of her naval, military, and industrial strength and her position athwart the world's trade routes to expand into a great commercial world power. The contest was fought primarily between groups of Whigs—no Tories held any governmental office of importance after the accession of George I. Although they occupied from one-fifth to one-fourth of the seats in the House of Commons, they seldom took much of a direct hand in the shaping of national policy, generally throwing their weight, however, when they did intervene, on the side of isolationist rather than internationalist tendencies.

A bitter struggle for power at once developed between the internationally minded Lords Stanhope and Sunderland (Marlborough's son-in-law) on the one side, and Robert Walpole and his brother-in-law Lord Townshend on the other. The Townshends and Walpoles were originally Norfolk country gentry, and Walpole never lost touch with the feelings and values of the squirearchy; indeed the Tory country gentlemen in Parliament saved him from defeat on several occasions, and Samuel Johnson, who as a young man had written vitriolic invective against him, in the end came to admire him ("He was the best minister this country ever had; and if *we* would have let him, he would have kept the country in perpetual peace"). The much too enterprising financial schemes of the South Sea Company, with which the Sunderland–Stanhope administration was closely allied, ended in 1721 with the bursting of the South Sea Bubble— an enormous stock-market boom, in which prices of stocks, led by those of the company, were preposterously inflated, and then collapsed overnight, to the ruin of thousands of speculators, while a few officials of the company, acting in collaboration with members of the government, made fortunes. Stanhope and Sunderland both conveniently died at this time, leaving Walpole, who had been out of office and was not known to be connected with the South Sea Company's activities, in possession of the field.

Walpole's pacific foreign policy, supporting the Quadruple Alliance of Britain, France, Austria, and Holland, which was to ensure the continuance of the peace agreed on at Utrecht, his conservative financial policy at home, and his ruthlessness in getting rid of any colleague who showed signs of being a potential rival for his leadership—in succession, he forced such powerful figures as Townshend, William Pulteney, Lord Carteret, Lord Chesterfield, and the Duke of Argyll out of office—maintained him in office for twenty years, the longest term of any

British Prime Minister.[2] The ejected Whig leaders, however, formed a powerful opposition faction, to which were presently added Bolingbroke, permitted to return from exile in France; Frederick, Prince of Wales, always eager to thwart his parents, who approved highly of Walpole; and, most important of all, the Patriots, headed by William Pitt, grandson of the merchant prince Thomas Pitt. Determined that Britain should obtain a share of the lucrative South American and Pacific trade, hitherto a monopoly of Spain, this group clamored patriotically (that is, jingoistically) against that country, retailing such atrocity stories as that of the patriotic Captain Jenkins, master of a merchant vessel, who resisted the encroachments of the Spanish coast guard, who retaliated by cutting off his ear. Walpole weakly allowed himself to be forced into war against Spain (the War of Jenkins' Ear) and then conducted it feebly and unsuccessfully. He was finally forced out of office in 1742 to the accompaniment of denunciations as "the betrayer of British honor" and "the enemy of British commerce."

However, the Patriots, headed by Pulteney, Carteret, and Pitt, were unable to form, or unwilling to risk forming, an administration made up solely of their own supporters, and made a deal which resulted in a coalition with Walpole's supporters ("Patriotism is the last refuge of a scoundrel," Johnson commented.) For another fifteen years, Henry Pelham and his brother the Duke of Newcastle continued to conduct the government of the country in much the same cautious way as Walpole had done. But in the early 1750's, as French and English interests began to conflict more and more in India and in the Ohio Valley, Pitt once again embarked on a crusade for war, this time with far-reaching results. Forcing himself into a coalition with Newcastle, who was to look after the domestic scene while Pitt took charge of military and diplomatic affairs, he brilliantly conducted the Seven Years' War ("The Great War for the Empire") to a resoundingly successful close. Britain emerged from the Peace of Paris in 1763 the gainer by two subcontinents, Canada and India, with unsurpassed naval and military might, a huge war debt—which was shortly to cause trouble when a later Prime Minister, George Grenville, tried to get the American colonists, now freed from the threat of French aggression to the north and west, to pay part of it—and an irrevocable commitment to commercial and imperial expansion. Writers of these decades, Swift, Pope, Johnson, had seen clearly enough the direction in which Britain was heading, and warned of the dangers involved: the cost in bloodshed, in oppression of native populations, in the moral corruption of a policy which placed material gain above all other values, of a "patriotism" which proclaimed, with James Thomson, that Britain had arisen "at Heav'n's command" and been commanded to "rule the waves." But Thomson found more willing listeners than Swift and Johnson, and the course of Britain's destiny for the next two centuries had been determined.

From the Peace of Paris to the Beginning of the French Revolution: 1763–1789

Chronology: 1763–1789

1763   Bute resigns; George Grenville, Prime Minister, initiates policy of economy (and American taxation) to pay for war costs.

1765   Stamp Act passed; violently resisted in America. Grenville dismissed; Rockingham Prime Minister.

1766   Stamp Act repealed; William Pitt, Earl of Chatham, Prime Minister. Incapacitated, he withdraws from activity, and the Duke of Grafton becomes Prime Minister.

1769   Turmoil over John Wilkes's expulsion from the House of Commons.

1770   Lord North Prime Minister.

1773   American resistance to taxation continues (the Boston Tea Party).

1775   Military actions between British troops and Americans. Battles of Lexington, Concord, Bunker Hill.

1776   American Declaration of Independence.

1777   British army under Burgoyne surrenders at Saratoga.

1780   London mobs riot over proposed extension of Roman Catholic civil rights (the Gordon riots—led by Lord George Gordon).

1781   British surrender at Yorktown.

1782   North resigns; Rockingham, later Shelburne, Prime Minister.

1783   Peace of Versailles ends American War, with recognition of American independence.

1783   After brief coalition government of North and Charles James Fox, William Pitt the younger (aged twenty-four) becomes Prime Minister; retains office 1783–1801 and again 1804–1806.

1789   Summoning of the French States-General, and storming of the Bastille: beginning of the French Revolution.

Confusion and Consolidation

The myth perpetuated by the American Declaration of Independence that George III was a tyrant, trying to turn the clock back to the days of royal absolutism, has long been discredited by responsible historical investigation.[3] He was an immature, inexperienced, conscientious young man who had been brought up in the Patriot tradition of his father, Prince Frederick, and he felt it his duty, on ascending the throne, to try to put into practice the high-sounding principles to which the Patriots gave noisy lip service. Others, like Samuel Johnson, who had been taken in for a time by the lofty ideals they professed, were thoroughly disillusioned when, after Walpole's downfall in 1742, the opposition leaders showed themselves as eager for the spoils of office as any Walpolian. But young George, carefully insulated from political reality by his mother, Princess Augusta, and his tutor, Lord Bute, managed to preserve his idealistic innocence, and when he ascended the throne in 1760, he resolved that the government of the country should no longer be a monopoly of the self-seeking politicians of the Walpole–Pelham–Rockingham faction, which had been in power so long, but should be guided for the good of the country as a whole by a king and ministers who should be "above party." [4] The Whigs of the Walpole tradition, guided by their chief propagandist, Edmund Burke (especially in his influential *Thoughts on the Present Discontents,* 1770), maintained that this cry of nonpartisanship was merely an astute device to hoodwink the public while its advocates (whom Burke termed "the King's friends") unconstitutionally seized power and ruled the country from behind the scenes, in the King's Cabinet. This might very well have been an accurate description of the real motives, conscious or unconscious, of such a Patriot as Bolingbroke; but young George certainly thought it possible to have a nonpartisan, unself-seeking executive. He failed, of course; but the bewildering series of ministerial changes that took place in the first ten years of his reign are testimony to the sincerity of his illusion.

The charge of tyranny made against George is given color for later students by the amount of public clamor that took place against various acts of his administrations. In fact, George's simple and virtuous domestic life and his transparent honesty made him perhaps the most popular sovereign England has ever had —the most popular, certainly, between Charles II and George V; and how accurately he could sometimes judge his subjects' political views was made clear in the general election of 1784, when the younger Pitt, whom George had forced on a hostile House of Commons, was overwhelmingly endorsed by the electorate. The fact was that, as the century progressed, the British public, becoming more and more literate and instructed in affairs of state by journalists like Johnson, was beginning to feel the desire to make its voice heard more loudly than hitherto. The outcome of this movement was to be the Reform Act of 1832 and the subsequent legislation which eventually established virtually universal suffrage in national elections. The sporadic outbursts of petitioning and the passing of resolutions by county associations and large public meetings in the early decades of George's reign were testimony to the development of this desire (and, of course, of the ease with which the public voice could be manipulated by shrewd politicians),[5] rather than to a greater desire on the part of George III than of his predecessors to "thwart the people's will."

Much nonsense has been written about the Wilkes affair being "a stalwart defence of democratic principles against encroachment by the Crown," and the like. Wilkes, a likable but thoroughly unscrupulous amateur in politics—he himself, as he said, was no Wilkite, and probably embarked on the enterprise in order to retrieve his personal fortunes—was voted by the House of Commons unfit, because of his unsavory record, to sit in that House. He was nevertheless reelected to it three times by the voters of Middlesex, to the accompaniment of much public uproar, whereupon the House declared his opponent to have received the larger number of *valid* votes (since Wilkes was ineligible) and to be the new member for Middlesex. A subsequent Parliament permitted him, however, to take his seat. In spite of historians, the incident in no way affected the right which the House of Commons still insists on to determine its own membership. In the twentieth century it has continued to invalidate elections of those who have received the largest number of votes in a constituency (for instance, Irish nationalists) and to declare their "defeated" opponents elected.

George III's reign began with the nation engaged in the concluding stages of the Seven Years' War. As usual in British history, the administration which had conducted a war was not the one which concluded the peace. Pitt, wishing to pursue and extend the war, but opposed by the rest of the Cabinet, resigned in 1762. Old Newcastle was likewise maneuvered into resigning—for all the stories told by Horace Walpole and others of his ineptness and love of intrigue, he had given the country faithful service for half a century, and spent a considerable fortune while doing so. George's mentor, Bute, was thus left without competition as First Minister. The Peace of Paris which he concluded was, however, unpopular (as most Peaces have been), and, unable to endure the scathing attacks made on him as a Scot, an outsider, and (allegedly) the lover of the Princess of Wales, George's mother, he too resigned in 1763. He was replaced by Pitt's brother-in-law, the conscientious but rigid George Grenville. He, however, annoyed the King by his pompous manner toward him, and the Americans by putting through the Stamp Act of 1765, a light but irritating tax on legal documents in the colonies, in an effort to meet part of the cost of the war, and George gladly parted with him the same year.

The King was then forced for a short time to put up with Lord Rockingham, now the leader of the old Walpole–Pelham Whig "connexion," which, under the guidance of Rockingham's secretary, Burke, was beginning to insist that it alone was the sole repository of simon-pure Whiggism, and that all other Whigs were really Tories in disguise. (This is a routine tactic of political propagandists, analogous to that of right-wing American political groups in the 1950's labeling President Eisenhower a crypto-Communist, but it nevertheless has taken in a good many later students; Grenville, North, and the Pitts considered themselves at least as good Whigs as the Rockinghamites.) George and Bute would probably have welcomed the accession of some good Tories to the Court (that is, the support of the administration), but true to their stubborn predilection for independence and opposition, few real Tories came. The Rockingham administration repealed the Stamp Act, which had aroused so much fury in America, but at the same time passed a Declaratory Act, maintaining the constitutional right of the British Parliament to impose taxes on the colonists if it chose. Rockingham's support in Parliament, however, was weak; he resigned in 1766, and Pitt, now the Earl of Chatham, became nominal head of the ministry. But his erratic health (mental as well as physical) caused him to abdicate his responsibilities, and after a short and unhappy period under the inexperienced and incompetent Duke of Grafton, the young Lord North emerged as the strongest figure in the ministry, and, to everyone's surprise, retained the Prime Ministership for twelve years, until 1782.

North, a charming and tactful personality, the heir of a family eminent for its intellectual and artistic interests, and a competent and industrious administrator, succeeded in giving Britain a reasonably stable government, and might have gone down in history as one of her most successful Prime Ministers if it had not been for the dispute with the American colonists. But probably no other British politician available at the time would have handled the situation any better. The trouble was that, thanks to Chatham and the Seven Years' War, Britain had suddenly become an imperial power before she was fully prepared to grasp the responsibilities that that position entailed.

Freed from the French military threat on their northern and western boundaries, the Thirteen Colonies, now containing a population of three million and filled with the same eighteenth-century spirit of enterprise that inspired their cousins in Britain, were obviously not going to rest content with their older status of small and negligible dependencies of the British Crown, but were going to insist on a large share of power in determining their own destinies. Nor did the British on the whole much wish to hamper them in doing so—they were occupied with their own problems. Even Johnson, whose *Taxation No Tyranny* (1775) was one of the most anti-American statements of the time (even the North government insisted that it be softened from its original form), is not really reluctant to "whistle them down the wind," as he misquotes *Othello*. What did bother him, of course, and what bothered Grenville, was the inability of the British taxpayer to recover from the Americans at least some of the very large sums of money expended in freeing the American colonists from the French threat and enabling them to expand westward. That, and the appalling amount of cant found in American patriotic publicity of the time, as in patriotic publicity of most times: "Why is it that we hear the loudest yelps for 'liberty' from the drivers of Negroes?" Johnson shrewdly asks, glancing at men like Patrick Henry and Thomas Jefferson.

What strikes the modern student about the events leading up to the Declaration of Independence in 1776 is the lack of any conscious design by the British to oppress the colonists. Things were allowed to drift through sheer inertia and lack of thought or planning. It was characteristic that the Secretary of State for the Colonies in 1775 should have been the most notoriously inept soldier and politician of the century, Lord George Germain, who in 1760 had been declared by court martial unfit to serve in the British army in any capacity. A century later, after Britain had had more experience in the role of an imperial power, ministers and civil servants might have been found who would have been able to handle such a situation sensibly and tactfully, as, in fact, the relations of Britain with Canada, when that country developed to the stage the Thirteen Colonies had reached in 1776, were handled. As it was, the separation took place in a way that left the utmost resentment on both sides, to the detriment of the future course of history.

The breaking away of the Thirteen Colonies did not result at the time in any great damage to British power. On the contrary, by providing some useful lessons in naval and military administration, and a healthful shock to its complacency, it probably strengthened Britain in the great struggle that was to come with Revolutionary France and Napoleon. The failure of British arms to subdue the colonists at last caused North to resign; he had long wanted to do so, but the King, fearful of what might happen if he lost him, persuaded him to continue. By this time, three fairly distinguishable parties of Whigs were emerging: those led by North, those led by the intellectual Earl of Shelburne, Chatham's political heir (though the younger Pitt was soon to supersede him), and those led by Charles James Fox, supported by Burke. The Tory independents, who had given somewhat reluctant support to North, deserted him when it became apparent that his policy in America had failed. When he resigned, Rockingham succeeded for a few months in keeping Shelburne and Fox together in the one ministry; but on his sudden death in 1783, the hostility between the two erupted, and Fox went into opposition, leaving Shelburne to act as Prime Minister and conclude the peace with the new United States. Shelburne, with young Pitt as his Chancellor of the Exchequer, was presently ousted when Fox and North, who had long been deadly enemies, announced that they had formed a coalition to take over the government.

The general disgust at this seeming cynicism enhanced the position of Shelburne and Pitt. This was reinforced by the introduction of Fox's India Bill, which would have placed the supreme control of the great subcontinent irrevocably in the hands of a few of his and North's supporters. In spite of the great majority which Fox and North together commanded in the House of Commons, George boldly dismissed them and appointed Pitt, then aged twenty-four, his Prime Minister. Fox and the rest angrily denounced this action as a flouting of the "popular will." But when a general election was held in 1784, Fox's supporters were disastrously defeated, and it was seen that the King had, in fact, been perfectly expressing the popular will by his appointment of Pitt, who remained in office, with a short break, for another twenty years. Pitt, the disciple of his father and of Adam Smith, succeeded during his first decade in office in building up Britain's economic and military potential to the point where she was able to endure successfully the long struggle with Revolutionary and Napoleonic France and enter the nineteenth century as a more formidable power than she had ever been before.

NOTES TO CHAPTER TWO

1. The youthful charm of "Bonnie Prince Charlie" has often been made the subject of romance. But his opponent and the victor at Culloden, William, Duke of Cumberland, George II's younger son, was exactly the same age—twenty-five.

2. The term "prime minister" is convenient to use here, but strictly speaking it is anachronistic: it did not come into even unofficial use until the nineteenth century, and was not given official recognition until the twentieth. Before the reign of George I, the most powerful minister was usually the Lord Treasurer; Walpole and his successors were usually, but not always, First Lords of the Treasury (i.e., chairmen of the commissions appointed to execute the office of Lord Treasurer).

3. The student will find a good brief statement of the modern view of the political structure of the time in the first chapter of J. Steven Watson, *The Reign of King George III* (Oxford: The Clarendon Press, 1960), in the Oxford History of England series.

4. The story told by Horace Walpole that George and his mother, the Princess of Wales, were directly influenced by Bolingbroke's *The Patriot King* was discredited by Romney Sedgwick in his introduction to *Letters from George III to Lord Bute, 1756–1766* (London: Macmillan, 1939). The "nonpartisanship" advocated by Bolingbroke was an old cliché, part of the standard equipment of opposition orators. Before Burke defended it, the concept of political party was like sin—everyone was opposed to it in theory, though seldom in practice.

5. See Herbert Butterfield, *George III, Lord North, and the People* (London: G. Bell, 1949).

❦ Three

Ideas and Attitudes

1660   The Royal Society founded; chartered by Charles II in 1662.

1661   Robert Boyle, *The Skeptical Chymist* (1662, announcement of Boyle's Law).

1663   Samuel Butler, *Hudibras:* the popular picture of Puritanism.

1667   Thomas Sprat, *History of the Royal Society,* with Cowley's *Ode to the Royal Society* prefixed.

       John Milton, *Paradise Lost.*

1678   Ralph Cudworth, *The True Intellectual System of the Universe* (Cudworth is often classified as one of the "Cambridge Platonists").

       John Bunyan, *The Pilgrim's Progress.*

1681   Thomas Burnet, *Telluris Theoria Sacra (The Sacred Theory of the Earth);* an important pioneering, if speculative, work of geology, with its theological implications.

1682   Richard Simon, S.J., *A Critical History of the Old Testament,* tr. Henry Dickinson; pioneering work in Biblical textual criticism; the occasion for Dryden's *Religio Laici.*

1687   Sir Isaac Newton, *Philosophiae Naturalis Principia Mathematica* (Newton's laws of motion, the foundation of classical physics and astronomy).

1689   John Locke, *Epistola de Tolerantia;* the first of three letters in defense of the principle of religious toleration.

1690   John Locke, *An Essay Concerning Human Understanding* (the basic statement of Lockean epistemology and psychology); *Two Treatises of Government* (his enormously influential political theory).

       Sir William Temple, *Essay upon the Ancient and Modern Learning* (opening of the battle of the Ancients and Moderns in England).

       Sir William Petty, *Political Arithmetick;* pioneering work in economics and statistics (written in 1670's).

1692   First Boyle Lectures in defense of Christianity delivered (by Richard Bentley; later lectures included Samuel Clarke's *Discourse Concerning the Being and Attributes of God,* 1704–1705).

1695   *The Post Boy,* the first successful daily newspaper, founded.

1696   John Toland, *Christianity Not Mysterious;* an important early Deist statement.

1699   Richard Bentley, *A Dissertation upon the Epistles of Phalaris;* the crushing answer to the proponents of the Ancients.

    Third Earl of Shaftesbury, *An Inquiry Concerning Virtue* (collected in *Characteristics,* 1711).

1702   Archbishop William King, *De Origine Mali;* tr. Edmund Law, later Bishop of Carlisle, as *An Essay on the Origin of Evil,* 1731, with a "Preliminary Discourse" by Rev. John Gay, adumbrating Utilitarian views.

    Edward Hyde, Earl of Clarendon, *A History of the Rebellion and Civil Wars in England.*

1704   Sir Isaac Newton, *Opticks;* the physics of light.

    Jonathan Swift, *A Tale of a Tub* and *The Battle of the Books* (written about 1697).

1705   Bernard Mandeville, *The Grumbling Hive;* expanded as *The Fable of the Bees,* 1714.

    George Hickes, *Linguarum Veterum Septentrionalium Thesaurus;* pioneering investigation of old Germanic literature and antiquities.

1710   George Berkeley, later Bishop of Cloyne, *A Treatise concerning the Principles of Human Knowledge.*

1717   Benjamin Hoadly, Bishop of Bangor, *The Nature of the Kingdom or Church of Christ* (a sermon; its alleged Erastianism precipitated the Bangorian Controversy).

1718   Lady Mary Wortley Montagu introduces inoculation for smallpox from Turkey.

1724   Bishop Gilbert Burnet, *A History of My Own Time* (to 1734); the standard Whig view of the reigns of Charles II, James II, and the Revolution.

1725   Francis Hutcheson, *An Inquiry into the Original of our Ideas of Beauty and Virtue;* an important statement of "benevolist" or "moral sense" ethical theory.

1726   Jonathan Swift, *Gulliver's Travels.*

1728   Alexander Pope, *The Dunciad* (later, much expanded and revised versions in 1729, 1742, 1743).

    William Law, *A Serious Call to a Devout and Holy Life.*

1731   *The Gentleman's Magazine,* the first magazine, founded.

1733   Pope, *An Essay on Man.*

1736   Bishop Joseph Butler, *The Analogy of Religion, Natural and Revealed, to the Constitution and Course of Nature;* regarded as the definitive answer to Deism.

Bishop William Warburton, *The Alliance Between Church and State: or the Necessity and Equity of an Established Religion.*

The obsolete laws against witchcraft repealed.

1739   David Hume, *A Treatise of Human Nature.*

1748   Hume, *Philosophical Essays* (including "Of Miracles").

1749   Lord Bolingbroke, *On the Idea of a Patriot King.*

David Hartley, *Observations on Man.*

1750   Montesquieu, *The Spirit of the Laws,* tr. Thomas Nugent.

1750's   Benjamin Franklin's experiments with electricity reported in *Philosophical Transactions* of the Royal Society.

1752   Jean Jacques Rousseau, *A Discourse on the Question of Whether the Revival of the Arts and Sciences Has Contributed to Purify Our Morals,* tr. R. Wynne.

1754   Hume, *A History of Great Britain* (later retitled *A History of England*); to 1762.

1757   Soame Jenyns, *A Free Enquiry into the Nature and Origin of Evil.*

1759   Voltaire, *Candid: or, All for the Best* (and several other translations of *Candide*).

Samuel Johnson, *The Prince of Abissinia* [*Rasselas*].

1763   Thomas Reid, *An Inquiry into the Human Mind on the Principles of Common Sense;* earliest of the Scottish "Common-Sense" school of philosophy, opposed to Hume.

1765   Sir William Blackstone, *Commentaries on the Laws of England* (to 1768); his lectures as Vinerian professor of law at Oxford; for a century or more the standard introductory textbook of English law.

1766   Henry Cavendish discovers the element hydrogen.

1770   Edmund Burke, *Thoughts on the Present Discontents;* beginning of the Whig interpretation of eighteenth-century British political history.

1772   Lord Mansfield, Lord Chief Justice, rules, in the case of Somerset, a Negro slave brought from Jamaica, that slavery can not exist on English soil.

1774   Joseph Priestley isolates oxygen.

1776   Adam Smith, *The Wealth of Nations.*

Edward Gibbon, *The Decline and Fall of the Roman Empire* (to 1788).

Jeremy Bentham, *A Fragment on Government;* a severe attack on Blackstone, adumbrating the Utilitarianism of the next century.

1781 Sir William Herschel, later Astronomer Royal, discovers the planet Uranus.

1787 Society for the Suppression of the Slave Trade founded by William Wilberforce and Thomas Clarkson.

1790 Edmund Burke, *Reflections on the Revolution in France.*

1791 Thomas Paine, *The Rights of Man;* the famous answer to Burke.

1794 Archdeacon William Paley, *A View of the Evidences of Christianity,* propounding the "argument from design"; for decades the standard textbook of Christian apologetics in English schools.

Mary Wollstonecraft, *A Vindication of the Rights of Woman.*

1796 Edward Jenner practices vaccination.

1798 Rev. Thomas Malthus, *An Essay on Population.*

Introductory

The history of ideas is one of the youngest intellectual disciplines—only some three or four decades old, at least under that name—and is very far from being an exact science. Since the ideas current in any period are bewilderingly numerous and diverse, and since statistical methods for determining their incidence are not known and indeed hardly seem possible,[1] it is a fertile field for unsubstantiated guesswork and ingenious speculation. Many of the accepted notions about the intellectual climate of eighteenth-century Britain seem to stem from the early textbooks of English literary history, full of hastily conceived postulates and generalizations, brought out in the mid-nineteenth century. That such textbooks began to be produced and disseminated on a wide scale in the midst of the nineteenth century's hostile reaction to the art and manners of its predecessor was particularly unfortunate for the eighteenth century. Although scholars and critics of the mid-twentieth century pride themselves on having attained to a fresh appreciation of the time, it is disheartening to see how many modern studies still content themselves with uncritically rehearsing terms and phrases that can be traced back through a succession of literary histories to the inspiration of some obscure pioneer textbook writer of the 1850's or 1860's.

To begin with the most popular of these phrases: it must strike any student who reads the important literary documents of eighteenth-century Britain with clear eyes that it was *not* an "age of reason." Quite the contrary: reason, as signifying the power of the human mind, without external aid, to arrive at valuable knowledge, was seldom if ever in such disrepute. "Dim as the borrowed beams of moon and stars," Dryden begins his confession of faith, *Religio Laici,* "is Reason to the soul." "Reason, an *Ignis fatuus* of the mind," sneers the skeptic Rochester. "So very *reasonable,* so unmoved/ As never yet to love or to be loved," Pope condemns the cold-hearted Chloe. "Reason is, and ought always to be, the slave of the passions [i.e., emotions]," writes Hume, summing up the whole tendency of the great British school of empiricism which dominated the philosophy of the century.

If the phrase means that, in fact, the average Englishman behaved, or tried to behave, more reasonably than his counterpart in other centuries, the history of the time, from the panic over the Popish Plot in 1678, through the South Sea mania in 1720, to the Gordon Riots in 1780—and much else in between—will give it the lie. As for the evidence of biography, few of the great figures of the time seem to have been models of emotional decorum and restraint: certainly not Swift, Pope, and Johnson; certainly not such politicians as Bolingbroke and the elder Pitt (whose performances in Parliament were masterpieces of melodrama); nor even such notable members of the traditionally stiff-lipped military profession as the volatile Lord Peterborough and the fervent, uninhibited Nelson. Perhaps the only literary figures whose writings come readily to the mind as exemplifying balance and judiciousness are such minor ones as John Evelyn and Lord Chesterfield. And even Evelyn had his infatuation with Mrs. Godolphin, and the deep neurosis that informs Chesterfield's obsession about the manners of his illegitimate son is readily apparent.[2]

Nor are other phrases that have been coined, or entities that have been postulated, to characterize eighteenth-century Britain more satisfying. There is "neoclassicism"—did writers and thinkers of the time really hold the Latin and Greek classics in greater awe or feel a greater obligation to use them as models for their own works and ideas than did Englishmen of earlier or even later centuries? It is true that a knowledge of the classics and a respect for them were among the hallmarks of any Englishman with pretensions to being educated from the Renaissance down to the beginning of the twentieth century. Yet it would be very hard to show that Dryden, Swift, Pope, and Johnson were more under the spell of the classic writers or that their own writings were more indebted to their example than, say, Spenser and Milton before their time, or Shelley and Tennyson after it. Is there really anything that resembles *Absalom and Achitophel* or *The Dunciad* or *Gulliver's Travels* or *The Lives of the Poets* in Latin and Greek literature? (Pope's and Johnson's "imitations" of Horace and Juvenal could no more be mistaken for Horace and Juvenal than Brahms's *Variations on a Theme by Handel* could be mistaken for Handel.) Like all great artists, Dryden and Swift and Pope did not think of themselves as "neo-" anything: they were attempting to do something new, something that had not been done before; and it is Johnson (whose own ways of writing and thinking are utterly unlike anything that had ever been done before or was to be done afterward) who most loudly applauds their originality, their invention, as an indispensable element of their genius.

"Augustanism," insofar as one can detect any meaning at all in this maddeningly opaque term, seems to imply that the writers of the time thought they were in the same towering class as Virgil, Horace, and Ovid were by comparison with lesser Roman writers of other times. The great admiration of Pope, Dryden, and Johnson for Shakespeare, Spenser, and Milton seems to rebut any such proposition. If it is meant to imply a complacent assumption that they lived in an imperial age, fit to give norms of behavior and thought to other times, the scathing indictments of their own age found in *The Secular Masque, The Dunciad* and Pope's later satires generally, and continually in Swift and Johnson, make it sound more like the age of Domitian than that of Augustus.

The term "the Enlightenment" (*die Aufklärung*), which is

often applied to the intellectual climate of the Continent, especially in the middle and late eighteenth century, seems at first glance to have more to commend it: certainly Pope, Swift, Johnson, and the rest were no friends of intellectual obscurantism. But the primary reference of the term is to the deism and atheism of the *philosophes,* Voltaire, Diderot, D'Alembert, and others: the enlightenment is above all the enlightenment of men's minds from the superstitions of institutional Christianity. It would be a radical mistake to think that Dryden, Swift, Johnson, and the vast majority of the eminent writers of eighteenth-century England, who were sincere and convinced Christians, held this fundamental point in common with their French contemporaries.

"Humanism," a term which has recently attained some popularity in eighteenth-century English studies, is open to a similar objection: if used in a narrow sense, it can mean the stridently antireligious posture of a Swinburne ("Glory to Man in the highest; for Man is the measure of things!") or the Renaissance veneration of (pagan) classicism, attitudes which were alien to Dryden, Pope, Swift, and Johnson.[3] And if the term is broadened so as to mean merely a profound concern for the human condition, there are few great writers, from Aeschylus up through Dante, Chaucer, Shakespeare, and Milton to T. S. Eliot and James Joyce to whom it would not be equally applicable.

The Augustinian Ethic

If we abandon the attempt to find a single neat word or phrase with which to delimit the immense intellectual diversity of eighteenth-century British thought, we can nevertheless easily discover certain important constellations of ideas and attitudes that were undeniably widespread and influential among educated men of the time. One of these, at least, is extremely obvious. As a distinguished historian of ideas has commented,

> However one defines the Age of Reason, however revolutionary and anti-authoritarian one estimates its spirit to have been, it should be noted that neither the Roman Catholic nor the Anglican nor the Lutheran communions ceased their ministrations in 1750. More-

over, in England, men like Burke and Johnson and Goldsmith, as much earlier Pope and Addison, continued to believe in the religion and philosophy of their forefathers.[4]

To this list of English writers of the time who professed orthodox Christian belief (and often used Christian teachings as the material of their writings) could be added Dryden, Defoe, Steele, Young, Smart, Richardson, Fielding, Sterne, Cowper, Crabbe, and a host of others—most strikingly, perhaps, the Very Reverend Jonathan Swift, Doctor of Sacred Theology, priest and dean in the Church of Ireland, whose tombstone, by his own direction, terms him *"strenuum pro virili libertatis vindicatorem"*—"one who defended freedom with all his might." The two greatest British scientists of the age, Newton and Boyle, were devout Christians, as were two of its three greatest philosophers, Locke and Bishop Berkeley.

By comparison, the list of important British writers who unequivocally rejected orthodox Christian doctrine is a small one. Hume and Gibbon are the two who most readily come to mind. Prior, Gray, and Horace Walpole evince some skepticism, but keep rather quieter about it. (Gray presumably subscribed the Thirty-Nine Articles of the Church of England in order to pursue his career at Cambridge.) Then there is a nebulous border region inhabited by the Deists, notably Shaftesbury and Bolingbroke, who profess admiration for the Christian ethic while rejecting its theology, and by Blake, who invented his own theological terminology to expound an ethic not very different from that of the Gospel.

But it is evident, as one makes one's way through the writings of the standard authors of Enlightened England, that their view of man and his place in the universe and his destiny is essentially that of such earlier Christian writers as Spenser and Milton, Donne and Herbert, rather than that of Voltaire and Diderot. They are still writing for an audience thoroughly indoctrinated, from childhood onward, with the King James Bible, the Book of Common Prayer, the Articles, Creeds, and Catechism (and *The Whole Duty of Man* and, later, *The Pilgrim's Progress*)—as, of course, the great majority of educated Englishmen and Americans were until at least the late nineteenth century—and they, the writers, are equally well acquainted with them and accept their teachings whole-heartedly. Any attempt to explicate the intellectual history of the time, or to analyze the thinking of most of its influential writers, which does not take this fact into account is bound to be distorted and misleading.

To the contemporary readers of Pope, Swift, Johnson, and Fielding, intimately familiar with the Book of Common Prayer, it would have seemed a superfluous undertaking to try to expound the elements of the "anthropology," psychology, and ethics found in that document; but since twentieth-century students can no longer be assumed to have such familiarity, an attempt must be made to present them here. To distinguish the fundamental point of view of sixteenth- to eighteenth-century Anglicanism (and Protestant Nonconformity) from variant ones found at other times and in other communions, it may conveniently be termed that of "Augustinianism"—that which Augustine of Hippo (following on St. Paul) was the first to expound forcibly. The following account, from a very reputable modern handbook, is a reliable and useful one:

Augustinianism denotes the interpretation of Christian faith, especially with regard to the doctrine of sin and redemption, which has its origin in the teaching of Augustine. . . . In essence, Augustinianism affirms strongly the fact of original sin—that is, the state in which man finds himself because of the Fall of Adam. In Adam . . . the manhood which we all share is thought to have lost its relationship of communion and fellowship with God. The resultant alienation is passed on to all his descendants, whose situation is thus one of deprivation of the grace of God, and, in consequence, one of chaotic disordering of the will. To be alienated from God results in the human tendency toward self-assertion in contradiction to the will and plan of God. Man is therefore helpless to "save" himself, since his will is perverted at the very root.

In Christ, seen as the embodiment of Divine Charity, God acts to give his "fallen" creatures a new beginning. This is accomplished by Christ as the new and perfect Man in whom God establishes the principle of grace. To this we can only respond in faith, by the surrender of our wills to his. . . . Once man has been caught up into this new relationship, his will is freed. No longer possessed by original sin, he is in the state of grace. The drive to evil which yet abides in him is conquered only by God's active love. . . .[5]

The question of predestination—of election and reprobation —is, of course, also closely bound up in strict Augustinian teaching with the matter of original sin and grace. Illogical as it has seemed to thoroughgoing Protestants of the Calvinist tradition, there has been a tendency in the Church of England from the very beginning to pass over it lightly. This has been done on the authority of the somewhat vaguely worded Article XVII, and it is not a question with which English Christian literary figures of the eighteenth century (with the notable exceptions of Defoe and Cowper) have greatly concerned themselves.

Augustinianism, in the Anglican communion, centers then on the affirmation of man's inherent moral weakness, which he is unable to rectify merely through his own unaided efforts— which, indeed, he will never be able to eliminate completely, for he is destined always to be a sinner and to deserve God's just punishment. That punishment cannot be averted by the performance of stipulated good works; indeed, works performed by the unrepentant sinner with a view to assuaging God's wrath have, Article XIII affirms, rather "the nature of sin." [6] It can be averted only by the full emotional acceptance of the fact of one's own imperfection and of God's merciful and forgiving love, freely offered to the sinner. If this change of heart takes place, good works—and moral virtue—will automatically follow. But so long as he remains stubbornly attached to his pride in his own individual superiority as a human being, that change cannot take place; true humility is required. The most memorable exposition of the doctrine is the great parable of the "pious" Pharisee, who prayed, "God, I thank thee that I am not as other men are, extortioners, unjust, adulterers," and the humble publican who "would not lift up so much as his eyes unto heaven, but smote his breast, saying 'God be merciful to me, a sinner.' " "I tell you," Jesus continues, "this man went down to his house justified rather than the other: for everyone that exalteth himself shall be abased, and he that humbleth himself shall be exalted."

Only if the exaltation of the self—pride, the original sin in the Garden—is diminished, can the individual fulfill the Great Commandment, "Thou shalt love the Lord thy God . . . and thy neighbor as thyself." For pride, self-centeredness, inhibits love.[7] And the disguises of pride are multitudinous, concealing it from its victim in subtle and ingenious ways. Nothing would be easier for the publican, by contemplating his own "humility" approvingly and carrying it on self-consciously (like Uriah Heep), than to transform himself into a Pharisee in a minute fraction of a second. There is never any guarantee that outward behavior, however seemingly commendable, is not the product of Pharisaic motivation; only if the inward workings of the heart were known could we tell.

Hence the examination of motives, searching introspection, the need to stifle any hint of self-complacency we find in ourselves are the continual subjects, of exhortation by the Book of Common Prayer, the two books of Homilies, the sermons and other writings of the Anglican divines of the sixteenth and seventeenth centuries—and the staple of a great deal of the imaginative literature of the eighteenth century, from Defoe and Addison, through Fielding, Richardson, and Sterne, to Johnson and Cowper.[8] "Rend your heart, and not your garments," beseeches one of the introductory scriptural sentences read at the beginning of the Order for Morning and Evening Prayer. Others are: "The sacrifices of God are a broken spirit: a broken and a contrite heart, O God, thou wilt not despise"; "If we say that we have no sin, we deceive ourselves, and the truth is not in us"; "I will arise and go to my father, and will say unto him, Father, I have sinned against heaven, and before thee, and am no more worthy to be called thy son."

The services of Morning and Evening Prayer begin with the great General Confession, recited by the priest and the whole congregation: "Almighty and most merciful Father, we have erred and strayed from thy ways like lost sheep. . . . We have left undone those things which we ought to have done, and we have done those things which we ought not to have done, and there is no health in us; But Thou, O Lord, have mercy upon us miserable offenders." The Collects are insistent on our sinfulness and impotence: "Through our sins and wickedness, we are sore let and hindered"; "Almighty and everlasting God, mercifully look upon our infirmities"; "By reason of the frailty of our nature we cannot always stand upright"; "We put not our trust in anything that we do"; "Create and make in us new and contrite hearts, that we, worthily lamenting our sins, and acknowl-

edging our wretchedness, may obtain . . . forgiveness"; "Grant
. . . by continual mortifying our corrupt affections, we may be
[saved]."

The Litany, the General Confession of the Communion Service, the Homilies appointed to be read in Anglican churches—

> The Holy Ghost, in writing the Holy Scripture, is in nothing more
> diligent than to pull down man's vainglory and pride, which of all
> vices is most universally grafted in all mankind, even from the first
> infection of our first father Adam. And therefore we read in many
> places of scripture many notable lessons against this old rooted
> vice, to teach us the most commendable virtue of humility, how to
> know ourselves and to remember what we be of ourselves. . . . Let
> us all confess with mouth and heart, that we be full of imperfec-
> tions; let us know our own works, of what imperfection they be,
> and then we shall not stand foolishly and arrogantly in our own
> conceits, nor challenge any part of justification by our merits or
> works[9]

—have much to say to the same purpose. It is hard to see how,
except by an act of conscious rejection (such as we have no reason to suppose that Swift or Johnson or most of their contemporaries among English writers ever made), anyone exposed to
such doctrine week after week from earliest childhood, as the
vast majority of the population of England were throughout the
eighteenth century, could with conviction maintain either the
Stoic view that human nature in itself provides a *datum* for
morality, or the Pelagian one that man has some inherent good
in himself and can, simply by industrious effort, lift himself by
his moral bootstraps.

The great English moral writers of the sixteenth and seventeenth centuries set forth the same doctrine uncompromisingly:
Spenser—

> If any strength we have, it is to ill,
> But all the good is God's, both power and eke will;

Donne—

> I am a little world made cunningly
> Of elements, and an angelic sprite;
> But black sin hath betrayed to endless night
> My world's both parts, and, oh, both parts must die.

and

Reason, your viceroy in me, me should defend,
But is captived and proves weak or untrue;

other influential divines like Bishop Lancelot Andrewes—

Both heathen and holy writers do commend to us that saying
Γνῶθι σεαυτον ["Know thyself"] but in a diverse sense. The heathen
use it as a means to puff up our nature, that in regard of the ex-
cellency which God vouchsafed us above other creatures we should
be proud thereof; but Christian religion laboreth by the knowledge
of ourselves "to cast down every high thing that exalteth itself
against the knowledge of God" . . . *Hoc piarum mentum est, ut
nihil sibi tribuant* ["Augustine"— marginal note], "This is the part
of godly souls, that they attribute nothing to themselves" [10]—

the Reverend Henry Hammond, chaplain to King Charles I,
uncle and tutor to Swift's mentor, Sir William Temple—

I, not I alone, abstracted from Christ, nor I principally, and Christ
only *in subsidiis* . . . which deceitful considerations drew on Pela-
gius himself . . . but I, absolutely impotent in myself to any su-
pernatural duty, being then rapt above myself, strengthened by
Christ's perpetual influence, having all my strength and ability from
him, am then by that strength able to do all things myself [11]—

the fluent and popular Robert South—

[Fallen man] is, as it were, a new kind of species; the plague of man
has even altered his nature, and eaten into his very essential. The
passions rebel . . . the light within us is become darkness; and the
understanding, that should be eyes to the blind faculty of the will,
is blind itself. . . . So great is the change, so deplorable the degradation of our nature, that whereas before we bore the image of
God, we now retain only the image of man[12]—

the saintly Bishop Thomas Wilson, educated at Trinity College,
Dublin, a few years before Swift—

All these pretend to reason; and indeed God has given all men reason. But lusts and passions will corrupt and blind our reason.
. . . You see, Christians, what we are by nature, what men are capable of, what they *would* be, when God leaves them to themselves,
and to their natural corruption. . . . No man can change, can
mend a corrupt nature, by a reason and will that are both corrupt.[13]

This is the tradition in which Swift and Johnson (and their readers) were raised, and which they continue in their writings.

To the average secularly educated Western man of the late nineteenth and early twentieth centuries, the doctrines of original sin and the depravity of man became little more than curiosities, on the whole repulsive, from the dead past. The writings of Swift, Johnson, Pope (at least, the later, more mature Pope, who "stooped to truth, and moralized his song"), Cowper, and others, in which these doctrines are taken for granted, have therefore appeared to such students to be full of pessimism and misanthropy. The presence of these traits has been generally accounted for by biographical considerations—the writers were the victims of various interesting neuroses, and much use has been made of Freudian terminology to explain them.

But in fact such explanations are as much beside the point as they would be when dealing with the writings of Spenser, Milton, Donne, and Herbert. If pessimism means, as one supposes it does, despair for the possibility of human salvation, the word can be applied to the teachings of neither Donne nor Swift. Both of them well know, and allow the careful reader of their works to know, that the means of salvation are within the reach of the individual—the abasement of human pride and the cultivation of the capacity for love; difficult, no doubt, for the average human individual, but not impossible. If misanthropy means a hatred of human beings and a desire to see them suffer, the term is equally impossible of application. What the individual must do, however, is to strip himself of all illusory self-congratulation on his own high moral status. He must look with clear eyes at the cruelty and devastation which history has testified that his sinful pride has inflicted (and continues to inflict) on himself and his fellows, to turn in revulsion from it, examine his own failings which have made those horrors possible, and endeavor to correct them.

The Dunciad, Gulliver's Travels, The Vanity of Human Wishes, Robinson Crusoe, Tom Jones, Tristram Shandy, The Vicar of Wakefield, Night Thoughts, Jubilate Agno, The Task, Songs of Experience offer little support to the individual who has to sustain his ego by cultivating complacency and self-satisfaction in the thought of the superiority of the human race over the rest of creation (or of the individual over his fellows). They do so because their authors, like Augustine and Spenser and Donne before them, believe that it is precisely such complacency that is responsible for man's self-created miseries and that gets in the way of the attainment of genuine human happiness —that happiness which, as Johnson puts it in the conspicuously *un*pessimistic last line of *The Vanity of Human Wishes,* can be "made" (though not "found"), through the cultivation of mental health, hope, patience, and, above all, love.

Empiricism

Equally potent and widespread an influence on English thinking in the eighteenth century was the "new science" of the Royal Society, and the philosophical tradition underlying it— the great British empiricist tradition. First proclaimed by Francis Bacon, developed by Locke, Berkeley, Hume, and John Stuart Mill, this tradition continues to flourish in the work of Bertrand Russell, Gilbert Ryle, A. J. Ayer, and others in the twentieth century. Except for a brief eclipse by Hegelianism in the later nineteenth century, it has dominated British philosophical investigation for three and a half centuries. And never was this more true than in the eighteenth century, when Locke reigned virtually unchallenged, except by his successors, Berkeley and Hume, who felt that he had not gone far enough in an empiricist direction. British philosophy of the time sharply dissociated itself from contemporary Continental philosophy, where the theorizing of Descartes, Spinoza, and Leibniz, organized in "logical" fashion like that of Euclid and Aquinas, still gave testimony to their confidence in the power of the human mind, unassisted by observation, to juggle words so as to add to our stores of knowledge. It is their age, that of seventeenth-century Continental philosophy, which is properly characterized by the title given to a collection of their writings in a popular series, "The Age of Reason."

Empiricism—the word derives from Greek ἔμπειρος, "learned by experience"—is the converse of "rationalism": it insists that the prime, perhaps only, source of genuine knowledge is the individual's experience, gained through the senses, of the world outside himself.[14] It disputes the ability of human reason to attain knowledge through its own isolated activity unaided by such experience; in particular it disputes the effectiveness of "logic," of the great syllogistic system of discourse developed by Aristotle and the scholastics, to furnish useful knowledge.[15] As a corollary, it is "nominalist" in its attitude toward language: words have no magic qualities in themselves—the mere fact that a word is in use does not guarantee, as Plato seemed to think, that there must be, somewhere or other, a reality that it stands for—but are merely meaningless marks and noises, which acquire significance only as men arbitrarily associate sense data with them. Four aphorisms of Bacon's *Novum Organum*—the "new instrument" for attaining knowledge, superseding Aristotle's treatises on logic, the "Organon"—sum all this up:

> I. Man, being the servant and interpreter of Nature, can do and understand so much and so much only as he has observed in fact or in thought of the course of nature: beyond this he neither knows anything nor can do anything.
>
> IX. The cause and root of nearly all evils in the sciences is this—that while we falsely admire and extol the powers of the human mind we neglect to seek for its true helps.
>
> XII. The logic now in use serves rather to fix and give stability to the errors which have their foundation in commonly received notions than to help the search after truth. So it does more harm than good.
>
> XIV. The syllogism consists of propositions, propositions consist of words, words are symbols of notions. Therefore if the notions themselves (which is the root of the matter) are confused and over-hastily abstracted from the facts, there can be no firmness in the superstructure. . . .

"Experience," then, not "reason," [16] is the key word of the controlling philosophy of the intellectual life of eighteenth-century Britain. Perhaps never in history have the formal teachings of philosophers been more quickly and widely disseminated among their compatriots as those of Bacon in the seventeenth century and those of Locke in the eighteenth.[17] It is easy, of course, to see why the exaltation of experience should have struck a responding chord in the bosoms of the inhabitants of expanding, exuberant, energetic post-Renaissance England. The most notable outcome (or at least concomitant) of the Baconian philosophy was, of course, the institution of the Royal Society of London for Improving Natural Knowledge, chartered in 1662 by Charles II, and still one of the world's great scientific bodies. The spirit of Bacon and the Royal Society has been condemned (generally by nineteenth-century Romantics and ultramontanists) as materialistic, as wanting to place complete reliance for the attainment of human happiness on the satisfaction of man's material wants. No doubt some scientists, then as now, held such a creed (as have many nonscientists, including such churchmen as Dostoevsky's Grand Inquisitor). Yet if one reads the writings of Bacon and his admirers—Bishop Thomas Sprat and the Reverend Joseph Glanvill, for instance—it is hard not to conclude that they were much concerned with the alleviation of man's moral and psychological ills. These they attributed to his sinful pride in his own mental powers and absorption in his own self-constructed conceits, the remedy being the empiricist recommendation of scholarly humility and a willingness to make contact with experience outside oneself. The unhealthy mental and emotional life of the rationalist is scathingly described by Bacon:

> This kind of degenerate learning did chiefly reign amongst the schoolmen; who having sharp and strong wits, and abundance of leisure, and small variety of reading; but their wits being shut up in the cells of a few authors (chiefly Aristotle their dictator) as their persons were shut up in the cells of monasteries and colleges; and knowing little history, either of nature or time; did out of no great quantity of matter, and infinite agitation of wit, spin out unto us those laborious webs of learning which are extant in their books. For the wit and mind of man, if it work upon matter, which is the contemplation of the creatures of God, worketh according to the stuff, and is limited thereby; but if it work upon itself, as the spider worketh his web, then it is endless, and brings forth indeed cobwebs of learning, admirable for the fineness of thread and work, but of no substance or profit.

And, again, elaborating on the image,

> The men of experiment [i.e., "empirics" in the pejorative sense, aimless collectors of desultory facts] are like the ant: they only col-

lect and use; the reasoners resemble spiders, who make cobwebs out of their own substance. But the bee [the empirical scientist as Bacon conceives him] takes a middle course: it gathers its materials from the flowers of the garden and of the field, but transforms and digests them by a power of its own.[18]

Swift was later to take over these images in a famous passage in *The Battle of the Books* (1697; published 1704). True, it is the Moderns whom he charges with the spider's arrogant rationalism and the Ancients to whom he attributes the bee's humble empiricism,[19] as if to point out, what is true and very important, that the age you live in and the labels you affix to yourself are no guarantee of your mental and moral soundness. Nevertheless, it is Bacon's empiricism he is championing here against the spirit of rationalism (in the actual battle, Bacon escapes the general slaughter of the Moderns: Aristotle shoots an arrow at "the valiant Modern," but it misses him):

> Erect your schemes [says Aesop, the moderator, to the spider] with as much method and skill as you please; yet if the materials be nothing but dirt, spun out of your own entrails (the guts of modern brains) the edifice will conclude at last in a cobweb. . . . For anything else of genuine that the Moderns may pretend to, I cannot recollect; unless it be a large vein of wrangling and satire, much of a nature and substance with the spider's poison; . . . As for us the Ancients, we are content, with the bee, to pretend to nothing of our own, beyond our wings and our voice, that is to say, our flights and our language. For the rest, whatever we have got, has been by infinite labour and search, and ranging through every corner of nature; the difference is, that, instead of dirt and poison, we have rather chosen to fill our hives with honey and wax, thus furnishing mankind with the two noblest of things, which are sweetness [of the spirit] and light [of the intellect].

That the new science of the seventeenth century and Christianity were entirely congenial, its contemporary English apologists were profoundly convinced. Even the titles of their books proclaimed this—for instance, *The Christian Virtuoso: Shewing that by Being Addicted to Experimental Philosophy, a Man Is Rather Assisted, than Indisposed, to Be a Good Christian* (1690), by the great Robert Boyle, "the Father of Chemistry," formulator of Boyle's Law, and founder of the Boyle Lectures in defense of Christianity. There were two especially popular lines of argument. One, the "argument from design"—that the deeper insight provided into the ingenuity with which Nature works must convince us more thoroughly of the existence of an omniscient God who planned it all—carries less weight than it used to, perhaps because of its glib use in later times by Archdeacon Paley, of "Paley's watch" fame.

But the other argument deserves being considered more seriously than modern students of intellectual history have tended to do. In its simplest terms, it is that the moral and psychological basis of the "new philosophy," as of Augustinian Christianity, is the derogation of the inherent powers of human nature, in particular human reason. By adopting an attitude of humility as to what man can accomplish without external aid—in morality, from God; in science, from God's creation—one can learn both to love and to know. If this proposition is true, there is no need to marvel at Addison, in a fine hymn, hailing the discoveries of the great Newton (himself a fervent Christian),

> The spacious firmament on high,
> And all the blue ethereal sky,
> And spangled heav'ns, a shining frame,
> Their great Original proclaim:

or at the devout Samuel Johnson choosing as the epigraph for his most labored work of morality, *The Rambler,* the great "skeptical" and "anti-authoritarian" motto of the Royal Society, *Nullius addictus in verba magistri jurare*—"Committed to swearing by the words of no master."

That there was any inherent antagonism between science and religion, the problem that so worried the nineteenth century, the Christian thinkers of the eighteenth century seem to have been unaware; and it may well be that this was because their religious thinking was maturer and full of deeper insight than that of, say, Tennyson or Arnold. It might even be argued that it was closer to that of Barth, Bultmann, or Reinhold Niebuhr in the twentieth century who, seeking to purify religion of anthropomorphic and socially conditioned concepts, find the extension of scientific knowledge no cause for concern as tending to undermine genuine religious belief.

The most explicit apologist of the new science was the Right Reverend Thomas Sprat, Bishop of Rochester, Doctor of Divinity and Fellow of the Royal Society—a combination of honorifics commoner then than now. His arguments are worth attending to as indicative of the official position in the seventeenth and eighteenth centuries. His *History of the Royal Society,* a manifesto rather than a history, since the Society was a mere infant in 1667 when he published the work, contains sections headed "Experiments not dangerous to the Christian religion," "Experiments will not destroy the doctrine of the Godhead," "Experiments not injurious to the worship of God," "Experiments not prejudicial to the doctrine of the Gospel," and much else.

Two sections are of particular interest. One is "Experiments useful for the cure of men's minds": "If we shall cast an eye on all the tempests which arise within our breasts," he remarks, in a passage of which Samuel Johnson and a modern psychotherapist would thoroughly approve,

> and consider the causes and remedies of all the violent desires, malicious envies, intemperate joys, and irregular griefs by which the lives of most men become miserable or guilty, we shall find that they are chiefly produced by idleness, and may be most naturally cured by diversion. Whatever art shall be able to busy the minds of men with a constant course of innocent works, or to fill them with as vigorous and pleasant images as those ill impressions by which they are deluded, it will certainly have a surer effect in the composing and purifying of their thoughts than all the rigid precepts of the Stoical, or the empty distinctions of the Peripatetic, moralists.

Or to put it in modern terms, contact with reality is the best psychotherapy. And in "Experiments not prejudicial to [religious] mortification," replying to the charge that the empirical attitude toward life will hinder what "concerns that which is necessary to a holy life, the mortifying of our earthly desires," Sprat explicitly draws the parallel suggested above, between the humility advocated by the empirical scientist and the humility advocated by Augustinian Christianity:

> I will affirm that it is improbable that even the hardest and most rigorous parts of mortification itself should be injured by these

studies more than others; seeing that many duties of which it is composed do bear some resemblance to the qualifications that are requisite in experimental philosophers. The spiritual repentance is a careful survey of our former errors and a resolution of amendment. The spiritual humility is an observation of our defects and a lowly sense of our own weakness. And the experimenter for his part must have some qualities that answer to these: he must judge aright of himself; he must misdoubt the best of his own thoughts; he must be sensible of his own ignorance, if ever he will attempt to purge and renew his reason: So that if that be true, which is commonly observed, that men are wont to prove such kinds of Christians as they were before; and conversion does not destroy, but only exalt our tempers; it may well be concluded that the doubtful, the scrupulous, the diligent observer of Nature is nearer to make a modest, a severe, a meek, an humble Christian, than the man of speculative science, who has better thoughts of himself and his own knowledge.[20]

Abraham Cowley, the most renowned poet of the time, reinforces Sprat's teaching in his famous *Ode to the Royal Society* prefixed to Sprat's book, where he equates rationalism with the original sin of pride—

> Yet still, methinks, we fain would be
> Catching at the forbidden tree;
> We would be like the Deity
> When truth and falsehood, good and evil, we
> Without the senses' aid, within ourselves would see;

and praises Bacon's nominalism—

> From words, which are but pictures of the thought
> (Though we our thoughts from them perversely drew),
> To things, the mind's right object, he it [philosophy] brought.

To trace in detail the involved history of the development of British empiricist philosophy through Locke, Berkeley, Hume, and the rest is beyond the scope of this work. It is enough to notice that, whatever modifications and subtleties were introduced, the underlying assumptions remained the same— knowledge is acquired by observation, by sensory experience, of the world outside oneself; the human mind, unaided by such observation, is an impotent instrument, and the ingenious theories it is capable of weaving out of words in a vacuum are ludicrous and may be dangerous. " 'Words are the daughters of earth, and things are the sons of heaven.' Language is only the instrument of science and words are but the signs of ideas," [21] to quote a formulation of nominalism by that skilled student of words, Samuel Johnson.

Locke is not so thoroughgoing an empiricist as his successors, and is still influenced to some extent by the older rationalist view. His *An Essay Concerning Human Understanding* begins with the assertion, which Sprat and others would have found discouraging, that "it is the *understanding* that sets man above the rest of sensible beings, and gives him all the advantage and dominion which he has over them" and he talks of its "nobleness." Yet even he at once begins filing caveats: "the comprehension of our understandings comes exceeding short of the vast extent of things."

It is the great Bishop of Cloyne, however—it is worth while emphasizing Berkeley's position in the Church—who sharply corrects Locke's hankering after rationalism ("Is the human mind really capable of 'abstract ideas,' as Locke thinks? Can one really visualize an abstract 'triangle,' one that is neither equilateral, isosceles, or scalene?") and whose insistence on the supreme importance, epistemological and moral, of the vivid, direct perception of experience has so appealed to poets. "Look!" his Philonous cries to Hylas, who has been persuaded by Lockean arguments based on the metaphysical postulate of "substance" to doubt the evidence of his senses:

> Are not the fields covered with a delightful verdure? Is there not something in the woods and groves, in the rivers and clear springs, that soothes, that delights, that transports the soul? At the prospect of the wide and deep ocean, or some huge mountain whose top is lost in the clouds, or of an old gloomy forest, are not our minds filled with a pleasing horror? Even in rocks and deserts is there not an agreeable wildness? How sincere a pleasure is it to behold the natural beauties of the earth! [22]

Linked with this experientialist or existentialist epistemology is the remarkable pronouncement that Berkeley made in one of his (to be sure, very early) notebooks: "Sensual Pleasure is the Summum Bonum. This the Great Principle of Morality." [23] And of course, Berkeley maintains, he has devised his formulation of empiricism to support Christian belief: *A Treatise Concerning the Principles of Human Knowledge, wherein the chief causes of error and difficulty in the sciences, with the grounds of scepticism, atheism, and irreligion are inquired into* is the full title of his principal work. *Esse est percipi* ("To be is to be perceived") —existence, life, is experience; God is the creating and sustaining principle of life, the "ground of being":

> It is therefore plain that nothing can be more evident to anyone that is capable of the least reflection than the existence of God, or a Spirit who is intimately present to our minds, producing in them all the variety of ideas or sensations which continually affect us, on whom we have an absolute and entire dependence, in short "in whom we live, and move, and have our being."

When our minds erect a barrier of abstractions—words—between ourselves and experience—reality, God—we begin to introduce confusion and error into our intellectual and misery into our emotional lives.

It may be argued then that in the dominant religious teaching and the dominant philosophy of eighteenth-century Britain there are important common and mutually reinforcing elements which together form a kind of unformulated "ethic." A great many of the important writers of the time implicitly subscribed to this ethic; it underlies and makes intelligible their most important writings, from Bunyan's *The Pilgrim's Progress* to Goldsmith's *The Vicar of Wakefield* (and pushing ahead a little, to the novels of Jane Austen), and certainly including, say, Swift's *Gulliver's Travels* and *A Tale of a Tub,* Johnson's *Rasselas* and *The Vanity of Human Wishes,* and Sterne's *Tristram Shandy.* A crude formulation of some of its salient points might run as follows:

1. What is needed first of all is the willingness to abandon an irrationally exalted view of our own absolute importance—both as individuals and as a species—in the total scheme of things, and of our inherent capacity for moral and intellectual achievement without external aid; a willingness to see ourselves *sub specie aeternitatis* and to accept without resentment our built-in limitations. To do otherwise is tantamount to a complaint that

we are not God. The ideal would be the ability to forget completely the demands of that abstraction "the self," and to lose ourselves wholly in what is outside ourselves, in experience, in others. Being men, incurably burdened with the original sin of pride, we shall never succeed in attaining that ideal; yet we can always approach more closely to it.

2. We must perceive that, in view of our own imperfections and insignificance, concern for our *relative* status, pride in our superiority in some detail over some other creature, is pointless ("The Houyhnhnms . . . are no more proud of the good qualities they possess than I should be for not wanting a leg or an arm, which no man in his wits would boast of": the penultimate sentence of *Gulliver's Travels*). A spirit of competitiveness, of striving for "one-upness" among members of a uniformly imperfect creation, all infinitely below the perfection of its Creator, is thus ruled out as absurd to begin with—apart from the pragmatic reason that it is the cause of the self-inflicted human misery of which history recounts such a ghastly toll.

3. Rather than close our eyes and dwell on the internal fantasies created by our egos in their eternal striving for self-importance, we should develop our receptivity to the rich sources of delight and knowledge, moral as well as material, available through sensory experience. Such a heightened awareness is the prerequisite not only for obtaining the accurate information that enables us to make the best we can of our imperfect earthly existence in material terms, but for developing the capacity for genuine love of our fellow men.

4. We must beware of letting ourselves be taken in by words —by abstractions—which can so easily become vehicles of self-centered illusion, and must always be ready to check these noises, meaningless in themselves, against the concrete experience they are supposed to represent.

There is much more to this "constellation" of attitudes than this primitive sketch—though perhaps it would be unwise to try to reduce it to a more precise formulation—and of course it would be nonsensical to claim it as something peculiar to the English writers of the seventeenth and eighteenth centuries. It is possible to find this ethic implicit in Marlowe's *Faustus* and in Spenser, to take examples from the sixteenth century, and in the plays of Edward Albee and the novels of James Baldwin, to mention two very serious moralists of the twentieth century (who, like Swift, are condemned for the squalid and pessimistic view of humanity they present, as though any imaginative writer could equal in horror the historical reality of what human beings have inflicted on one another in the twentieth century, from Ypres and Verdun, through Belsen and Buchenwald, to Hiroshima and beyond). To provide examples from other literatures, one might name Rabelais (Swift's master) and Tolstoy. But it could perhaps be argued that the English climate of opinion of the eighteenth century was peculiarly favorable to such an ethic.

Deism, Stoicism, Laissez Faire

There were of course many deviant and heterodox positions besides this. Again it must be emphasized, however, that throughout the century these are distinctly minority views. Being minority ones, they naturally stirred up controversy, and so gained publicity for themselves, publicity which has inveigled later students into thinking that they were more widespread and influential than they seem to have been: one sometimes gets the impression from reading intellectual histories of the century that most of the English population were Deists or primitivists, and that there was hardly an orthodox Christian in the land. But on the evidence of the literature of the time, this is nonsense.

The heresy that made the greatest stir in the late seventeenth and early eighteenth centuries was Deism—the affirmation of the existence of a God (or, to use popular Deist expressions, a "Supreme Being" or an "Author of Nature"), while rejecting the need for revealed and institutional religion. Perhaps the best exposition of the Deist argument is given in Dryden's *Religio Laici;* indeed, Dryden states it so effectively that he is hard pressed to answer it in his poem, if it can be said that he answers it at all:

> No supernatural worship can be true:
> Because a general law is that alone
> Which must to all and everywhere be known:

A style so large as not this Book [the Bible] can claim, . . .
And what provision could from thence accrue
To Indian souls, and worlds discovered new?

It is understandable that in the seventeenth century, Europeans, becoming more vividly aware of the existence of millions of human beings in the center of Africa and South America, might well ask whether, unaware of the instruction provided by the Bible and the Church, their souls were therefore doomed to eternal damnation.

The Deist answer (first formulated, apparently, by Lord Herbert of Cherbury—George Herbert's brother—in his *De Veritate,* 1624) was that the ability to recognize the existence of God and to ascertain and obey his commandments must be innate in the human frame, whatever its environment; or, as Pope put it in *An Essay on Man,* 1733: "Lo, the poor Indian! whose untutor'd mind/ Sees God in clouds, or hears him in the wind." The inevitable question, "What need, in that case, for Scriptures, creeds, and a Church to expound them?" was carefully avoided by Herbert and Pope; but other bolder spirits ventured to hint at it—John Toland, in *Christianity Not Mysterious* (1696), Matthew Tindal in *Christianity as Old as Creation* (1730), Henry Dodwell in *Christianity Not Founded on Argument* (1742), and others.[24] Most of these writers, minor figures at best, received a rough reception at the hands of the orthodox, and certainly made few converts among the general public. They were the progenitors of later militant "freethinkers" like Tom Paine (whose *The Age of Reason,* 1793, implies that an age so burdened with religious superstition as the eighteenth century is anything but an age of reason—that is to come in the enlightened future) and Robert Ingersoll, objects of awe and curiosity rather than writers of much real influence.

A related controversy went on about miracles. The Anglican church rejected the modern "miracles" of countless Roman Catholic saints, but accepted those recorded in the Bible. Deists like Anthony Collins (*Discourse on Freethinking,* 1713) and Thomas Woolston (*Discourses,* 1729) gleefully accused the Anglicans of inconsistency; the Reverend Conyers Middleton, defending the Anglican position too lukewarmly, as it was thought, found himself suspected of heresy; but the last word was said by David Hume, whose devastating essay "Of Miracles" (1748) went deep into the fundamental epistemological question of why we should ever believe that any one thing is more likely to happen than any other at any time.

The Deist rejection of the need for revelation, or for formal instruction by a church, in order to know the ways and the will of God entailed (for those who retained the belief in the existence of a Supreme Being) the acceptance of "natural theology" —the doctrine that "Nature," or things as they are, can provide that knowledge. Among natural phenomena is human nature, which in its ideal, uncorrupted state, is assumed to be innately good and to possess the divine spark of reason, which is deemed innately capable of guiding man, by its own unaided power, to the true, the beautiful, and the good. This whole way of thinking derives from pagan Greek epistemology, psychology, and ethics, notably from Stoicism. As has often been pointed out (for instance, in A. O. Lovejoy's *The Great Chain of Being*), it implies a dualistic, rather than a monotheistic, theology. Nature, or the matter which constitutes it, becomes a God, equally powerful with the Supreme Being who is outside Nature; perhaps more powerful, since in some versions of natural law theory, it was maintained that God himself could not contravene the dictates of natural law. To the strictly orthodox, of course, all this was the most pernicious heresy, a denial of the First Commandment, "Thou shalt have no other Gods before me": Nature, including man's reason, was corrupted at the time of the Fall, and no moral norm can be taken from it. Nevertheless, because of the wide diffusion of Greek ideas in the Western world —Cicero, read in all schools as the best introduction to Latin prose, was a particularly fertile source of Stoic thought—it tended to infiltrate Christian thinking from Apostolic times onward.

The best known exponent of the Stoic view in the eighteenth century was Anthony Ashley Cooper, third Earl of Shaftesbury (grandson of Dryden's Achitophel, the first Earl, and ancestor of the seventh Earl, the noted humanitarian reformer and devout Evangelical of the nineteenth century). In his *Characteristics of Men, Manners, Opinions, Times* (1711), which brings together various earlier writings, Shaftesbury propounds, in windy, rhapsodical rhetoric, that Nature is a manifestation of a beneficent, if vague, Deity; that the contemplation of Nature is bound to lead to virtue, happiness, and right thinking; that men instinctively desire the good—indeed, that the Good and the Beautiful are essentially the same, so that the appeal of virtue to men is really an aesthetic appeal. It is true that, in practice, we very often find men attracted to evil rather than good; but this is because their primitive instincts have been corrupted by miseducation. It is easy to see how all this anticipates the teaching of the even more influential later primitivist, Rousseau.[25]

The definitive answer to those who maintained that revealed religion, with its alleged absurdities, should be replaced by the pure light of natural religion was given by Joseph Butler, Bishop of Durham, in his famous *The Analogy of Religion, Natural and Revealed, to the Constitution and Course of Nature* (1736), which argues that when the "course of nature" is actually inspected, it is quite as consistent with the operations of the God of revelation, as taught by orthodoxy, as with those of the Deists' Supreme Being—or, rather, as inconsistent with the God the Deists postulate as with the God of the orthodox. With either deity, there are difficulties. While it is true that revelation has not been bestowed on all men, neither has a Deistic God bestowed on all men equal intellectual ability to deduce moral principles from the universe around them. It is a dangerous line of argument: later men, contemplating a "Nature, red in tooth and claw," were to find it hard to believe that it was presided over by a benevolent God at all, whether Anglican or Deist. But at least Butler effectively establishes that there is no advantage in rejecting orthodoxy for a Deism which leaves just as many questions unanswered.

It is largely the Shaftesburians whom Johnson is pillorying in Chapter XXII of *Rasselas* (1759), where the young Prince of Abyssinia is much impressed by the philosopher who argues,

> The way to be happy is to live according to nature, in obedience to that universal and unalterable law with which every heart is originally impressed: which is not written on it by precept, but engraven by destiny, not instilled by education, but infused at our nativity. . . . Other men may amuse themselves with subtle definition, or intricate ratiocination. Let them learn to be wise by easier

means: let them observe the hind of the forest, and the linnet of the grove.

Johnson makes his point: it is a lazy man's philosophy. He also, interestingly, ties it up with its ancestral Stoicism: "He that lives according to nature," the philosopher asserts, "will suffer nothing from the delusions of hope, or importunities of desire: he will receive and reject with equability of temper." He will, that is, "in ignorance sedate,/ Roll darkling down the torrent of his fate"; as well as passivity of mind, the doctrine entails passivity of emotion, the sort of vegetable existence that Johnson could hardly bear to hear described. Finally, it is essentially arrogant and egocentric, another of the ubiquitous manifestations of the sin of pride. At the conclusion of the philosopher's harangue, Johnson makes a devastating observation: "When he had spoken, he looked round him with a placid air, and enjoyed the consciousness of his own beneficence." Shaftesbury does indeed argue that one of the rewards of virtuous behavior is the pleasant awareness of your own superior virtue, such as the Pharisee in the Gospels enjoyed.[26]

A specialized branch of natural theology was that devoted to answering the age-old question Πόθεν τὸ κακόν; what is the source of evil? How, if we postulate a God who is both omnipotent and benevolent (as both Christians and Deists did), can the existence of evil or pain in the world be accounted for? Either, it seems, God is unable to prevent it, in which case he is not omnipotent; or else he is able to but will not, in which case it is difficult to understand how he can be benevolent.[27] The standard treatise of the time on the subject was the *De Origine Mali* of William King, Archbishop of Dublin, (1702), later translated by Bishop Edmund Law as *An Essay on the Origin of Evil* (1731). King's answer is not a new one; it had made by Milton, among many others. It is an appeal to the theory of "the great chain of being," a concept whose origins Lovejoy traces back to early Greek philosophy.[28] All existence forms a hierarchical continuum, extending from God (infinity) at the top, down through the nine orders of angels, through man, who is somewhere in the middle, through the lower orders of animals, to the lowest forms of existence, and at last to zero. What seems evil to one member of the chain, then, may be for the good of another member, and for the good of the chain as a whole. Pope popularized the argument in *An Essay on Man:*

> God sends not ill; if rightly understood,
> Or partial Ill is universal Good,
> Or Change admits, or Nature lets it fall;
> Short, and but rare, till Man improv'd it all.
> We just as wisely might of Heav'n complain
> That righteous Abel was destroy'd by Cain,
> As that the virtuous son is ill at ease
> When his lewd father gave the dire disease.

("We" perhaps have no right to complain; but one wonders whether the syphilitic boy may not have some, or how much comfort he would derive from this line of argument.)

Soame Jenyns, a minor and dilettantish politician and writer, again attempted a popularization of it in his *Free Enquiry into the Nature and Origin of Evil* (1757), which would long ago have faded into oblivion if it had not caused Johnson to rise in his wrath and deliver a memorable onslaught on the whole way of thinking. The "great chain" concept is nonsense, Johnson says: between its highest finite member and the infinity of God there must continue to be an infinite interval; likewise between nonexistence and the lowest form of existence. The tendency of the whole line of reasoning is to keep the "have-nots" of the world (of whom Johnson had been one) contented with their lot and to leave the "haves" in untroubled enjoyment of their possessions: "Life must be seen before it can be known. This author and Pope perhaps never saw the miseries which they imagine thus easy to be borne." It is essentially dishonest reasoning, with the end justifying the means, and may even be malicious; to Jenyns' facile argument that ignorance is the desirable "opiate" (Jenyns' word) of the poor, of which they should not be improperly deprived by well meaning busybodies who want to educate them, Johnson retorts:

> I am always afraid of determining on the side of envy or cruelty. The privileges of education may sometimes be improperly bestowed, but I shall always fear to withhold them lest I should be yielding to the suggestions of pride, while I persuade myself that I am fol-

lowing the maxims of policy; and, under the appearance of salutary restraints, should be indulging the lust of dominion, and that malevolence which delights in seeing others depressed.

And Johnson sees quite clearly its derivation from Stoic dualistic theology, charging Jenyns with "dogmatical limitations of Omnipotence" and attempting to revive "Chrysippus's [the most seminal of Stoic philosophers] intractableness of matter."

The affinity of the doctrines of the *Characteristics,* the *De Origine Mali,* and *An Essay on Man* to the constellation of political attitudes termed laissez faire seems obvious. With whatever subtleties Pope and the others may have surrounded the affirmation "Whatever is, is right" in order to reconcile it with the orthodox view of the corruption of nature and human reason since the Fall (and with the experience of Johnson and others of the lower economic levels that whatever is is often very wrong indeed), to the average prosperous British entrepreneur of the eighteenth century it must have sounded like a ratification of free enterprise and a warning to meddling governments and moralists to keep their hands off the workings of the divinely established law of supply and demand. British merchants appealed in high-sounding terms to the wisdom of God as manifested in "the present order of things" when defending their "natural right" to infringe the Spanish monopoly of trade in the South Seas; so did Americans (as the Declaration of Independence testifies) when unwilling to be subjected to taxation by London; so even did defenders of the slave trade. Boswell, for instance, reprobates

> The wild and dangerous attempt which has for some time been persisted in to obtain an act of our Legislature, to abolish so very important and necessary a branch of commercial interest. . . . To abolish a *status,* which in all ages GOD has sanctioned, and man has continued, would not only be *robbery* to an innumerable class of our fellow-subjects; but it would be extreme cruelty to the African Savages [whom it] introduces into a much happier state of life.[29]

Locke's argument (in his *Second Treatise of Government*) that all society springs from the individual's need to protect the investment of his own labor in his own property, and his affirmation that the end of government is to preserve the individ-

ual's "life, liberty, and property"—with the stress on the last—
was of course also tremendously influential throughout the century, and beyond. But affluent and expanding societies seem
naturally to be the breeding ground of laissez-faire thinking:
the average person is reasonably prosperous, expects to become
more so, and is reluctant to have the economic terms which have
worked so well for him changed. God's in his heaven, all's right
with the world, and if other people remain poor, it is the result
of their own willful folly and laziness.

Bernard Mandeville's *The Grumbling Hive* (1705), a dog-
gerel poem of some four hundred lines, which, with long prose
appendices and replies to its critics, was later transformed into a
substantial volume entitled *The Fable of the Bees, or Private
Vices, Public Benefits* (1714), is certainly one of the most striking presentations of laissez-faire doctrine ever written, and was
the great *succès de scandale* of the early eighteenth century. It
tells of a hive of bees, "That liv'd in luxury and ease/ And yet
as famed for laws and arms"—England, in short—whose economy prospers because of the pride, greed, and emulation of its
inhabitants. The luxury trades flourish because of the desire to
keep up with the Joneses. Doctors become rich because of the
bees' self-indulgence and lawyers because of their striving to out-
cheat one another, and both do what they can to advance the
numbers and welfare of their own professions. So do the members of other trades, the slothful clergy, the cowardly soldiers,
the corrupt and teeming civil service. Vanity and fashion make
"built-in obsolescence" an essential feature of the economy:

> Their darling folly, fickleness,
> In diet, furniture, and dress,
> That strange ridic'lous vice, was made
> The very wheel that turn'd the trade.

So the gross national product remains at a high level, and everyone prospers: "the very poor/ Liv'd better than the rich before."

Then some moralistic busybody prays to Jove to remedy the
immorality of this affluent society, and Jove grants the prayer
and miraculously makes all the bees virtuous. They begin to
live honestly and sanely. Doctors, lawyers, even clergymen,
find no need for their services, and join the growing ranks

of the unemployed; the luxury trades are ruined; the expenditures of a government purged of grafting and ambitious politicians drop to new lows. But Mandeville knows that this picture of a plain living and high thinking society is not in itself going to fill his readers with too much alarm; some misguided moralists might even applaud it. So he makes the crucial addition: as well as other industries founded on immoral motivation, the military establishment decays:

> Vain cost is shunn'd as much as fraud;
> They have no forces kept abroad;
> Laugh at th'esteem of foreigners,
> And empty glory got by wars.

And, inevitably, the defenseless colony is at once attacked by aggressive neighbors eager to take advantage of its weakness. Mandeville does not quite have the courage to bring his tale to its logical conclusion, and show the foolishly virtuous community wiped out completely; its few courageous remnants, by dint of Spartan self-denial and self-sacrifice, beat off the invaders, saving it from annihilation. But in order to preserve it from future aggression, they have to emigrate from the conveniences of the hive, and "flew into a hollow tree,/ Blest with content and honesty." Translating this, the only solution would be for a society to isolate itself from the modern world and retreat into a primitive fastness—if such could be found, and it seems fairly certain that Mandeville does not think it can be.

Mandeville's argument is familiar in modern industrial (and advertising) circles. The spirit of emulation, waste, and conspicuous consumption is desirable, indeed essential, if industry is to be kept in so healthy a condition that, when need arises, it can quickly convert to effective defense production. It is usually said that Mandeville's book was an attack on Shaftesbury: insofar as it mocks Shaftesbury's admiration of the primitive life of nature, it is. But this is only an incidental part of Shaftesbury's teaching. In fact, Mandeville and Shaftesbury are basically in agreement: what both are saying, in effect, is "Trust human nature, and all will be well." Shaftesbury, to be sure, paints a different picture from Mandeville of what a laissez-faire world would look like, but both are satisfied that men do very well when left to the guidance of their own instincts. It takes a miracle by Jove to make Mandeville's bees "virtuous," and Mandeville is confident that no such miracle will take place. His "private vices" are intended not to be seen as vices at all, since they confer "public benefits"; moralists are wrong who label as vices material self-seeking and cutthroat competition with one's neighbors—these are the fundamental social and economic virtues. What both Mandeville and Shaftesbury are attacking, that is to say, is the orthodox Christian ethic, which maintains that human instincts are a very poor guide indeed and need constantly to be corrected by reference to a higher standard of conduct. The Christian answer to Mandeville is, of course, a very simple one: if the ultimate sanction for a vicious society is the need to sustain military power against aggression by other vicious societies, this is a further reason why the Christian ethic should be extended, not restricted, so as to eliminate the nationalistic pride and competitive spirit which makes such military action necessary.

Mandeville's book is slight, though far from insignificant either for his own or for later times. A much more weighty and influential work, of course, was Adam Smith's *The Wealth of Nations* (1776), for nearly a century and a half the Bible of "liberal" or "classical" or "Manchester school" economics. Smith, a Scottish academic of literary interests, would seem to have had no special qualifications for embarking on an economic treatise. His earlier book, *The Theory of Moral Sentiments* (1759), is a curious work, in which some of his data for a study of human motivation are drawn from the actions and speeches of the characters in the popular drama of the time, often not far removed in quality from modern soap opera. But it was a century when "every man was his own economist." The prevailing doctrine in pre-Adamite England (though not in France, where the physiocrats worked out a body of theory to which Smith was considerably indebted) had been for the most part what is called "mercantilism," in which the individual nation is regarded as a self-sufficient economic unit, and government action, in the way of protective tariffs, subsidies, and the like, is called for to keep the national economy healthy and balanced. Smith argues with great effectiveness that "free trade"— the removal of government controls on industry and commerce,

both internally and externally—is bound to lead to great pros-
perity. The natural "law of supply and demand" will see to it
that goods will find their proper price levels, and the full potential of the world's natural resources will be developed to the best
advantage of its inhabitants. There is no room here to consider
the many sharp critiques (notably Marx's) that were later made
of the classical economics that derived from Smith, and the bitter controversies that arose over it (and still go on). But it is
clear, at least, that, like all economic theories, it has profound
moral implications that cannot be ignored.[30]

The hints thrown out by Mandeville and Adam Smith were
to become dogma in the even more affluent Britain of the mid-
nineteenth century (where it was called "Liberalism"—that is,
freedom from government interference) and in mid-twentieth-
century America (where, confusingly, it is called "Conservatism"). It is also closely linked with the notion of inevitable
progress. Its classic formulation was by Macaulay in 1830:

> History is full of the signs of this natural progress of society. We
> see in almost every part of the annals of mankind how the industry
> of individuals . . . creates faster than governments can squander.
> . . . We see the wealth of nations increasing, and all the arts of life
> approaching nearer and nearer to perfection, in spite of the grossest
> corruption and the wildest profusion on the part of rulers. . . . It
> is not by the intermeddling of . . . the omniscient and omnipotent
> State, but by the prudence and energy of the people, that England
> has hitherto been carried forward in civilisation. . . . Our rulers
> will best promote the improvement of the nation by strictly confin-
> ing themselves to their own legitimate duties, by leaving capital to
> find its most lucrative course, commodities their fair price, indus-
> try and intelligence their natural reward, idleness and folly their
> natural punishment. . . .[31]

All this had been answered in advance by Goldsmith, who
puts the case for a strong, responsible, and enlightened central
government in Chapter XIX of *The Vicar of Wakefield:*

> [The great] who were tyrants themselves before the election of one
> tyrant are naturally averse to a power raised over them, and whose
> weight must ever lean heaviest on the subordinate orders. It is the
> interest of the great, therefore, to diminish kingly power as much as
> possible; because whatever they take from it is naturally restored to

themselves; . . . What they may then expect may be seen by turning our eyes to Holland, Genoa, or Venice where the laws govern the poor, and the rich govern the law. I am then for, and would die for, monarchy . . . every diminution of [the monarch's] power . . . is an infringement upon the real liberties of the [people].

Swift, Pope, and Johnson are very much on the same side as Goldsmith, and are equally skeptical that uncontrolled economic enterprise will lead to the Utopia that Macaulay foresaw. What has been called "the gloom of the Tory satirists"—and it is an oversimplification of contemporary political terminology to label Pope and Swift Tories—is no more than a gloom about what may happen in a community where "leaving capital to find its most lucrative course" becomes the highest political (and therefore moral) principle.[32]

NOTES TO CHAPTER THREE

1. Apart from the elementary one of counting the number of books published on a certain topic and attempting to estimate the number of their readers. Even this will hardly be feasible for the eighteenth century until a Short Title Catalogue of publications is extended beyond the present limit of 1700.

2. "Reason" has been supposed to connote a fondness for "logical structure" in the writings of the time. But see my article " 'Logical Structure' in Eighteenth-Century Poetry," *Philological Quarterly*, XXXI, 2 (July 1952) 315–336.

3. To Johnson in particular, who frequently sneered at the praise given by historians to the Romans and their empire—"a people, who while they were poor robbed mankind, and as soon as they became rich, robbed one another" (review of Blackwell's *Memoirs of the Court of Augustus*)— and whose scathing comments on the use of classical mythology and hackneyed classical literary conventions (e.g., by Milton) are one of the commonplaces of his criticism. Swift can—mildly—recommend the reading of the Greek philosophers, as a limited source of useful instruction; but his considered opinion of them is given in his sermon on the text "The wisdom of this world is foolishness with God," a sustained attack on them from Socrates onward: "this vein of affecting to raise the reputation of those sages so high, is a mode and a vice but of yesterday, assumed chiefly, as I have said, to disparage revealed knowledge, and the consequences of it among us." Swift and Johnson never forgot that the Greeks and Romans were, after all, heathens. Dryden did not hesitate (in *An Essay of Dramatic Poesy*) to express his admiration of the drama of Shakespeare and his contemporaries, for all its flouting of the conven-

tions of classical drama, nor was Pope reluctant to use the conventions of the classical epic as material for broad humor in *The Dunciad*. Certainly they all admired good classical literature, but they were far from being overawed by it.

4. George Boas, "In Search of the Age of Reason," in Earl R. Wasserman, ed., *Aspects of the Eighteenth Century* (Baltimore: Johns Hopkins, 1965), p. 18. The false dichotomy between religion ("authoritarian") and rationality ("anti-authoritarian"), found in so many attempts to view the century (in England) as the age of reason, is readily apparent in this passage. But there is nothing counterrevolutionary or authoritarian in the teachings of the Gospel when taken seriously, as presumably some, at least, in the Roman Catholic, Anglican, and Lutheran communions took them. One thinks of the toast of that devout Anglican, Samuel Johnson, "Here's to the next insurrection of the Negroes in the West Indies" (Boswell, *Life*, 23 September 1777). In the Roman Catholic church, the eighteenth century saw the pontificates of Benedict XIV, a worthy predecessor of John XXIII, and of Clement XIV, who dissolved the Jesuit Order: it might be argued that the *aggiornamento* of that church in the twentieth century is merely a rejection of the ultramontanism of the nineteenth century and a return to its eighteenth-century tradition. But Boas' essay is virtually an announcement of the abandonment of that search by one of the most senior and eminent historians of ideas.

5. W. Norman Pittenger (Professor of Christian Apologetics in the General Theological Seminary, New York), "Augustinianism," in *A Handbook of Christian Theology* (New York: Meridian Books, 1958), pp. 22–23. Other contributors to the volume include such distinguished theologians as Paul Tillich, Reinhold and H. Richard Niebuhr, and W. A. Visser 't Hooft. "Paulinism" would be an equally valid designation; so perhaps would "Erasmianism"—see J. K. McConica's *English Humanists and Reformation Politics* (New York: Oxford University Press, 1965), Chap. 2. McConica sums up Erasmus' teaching thus: "Above all, Christianity is to be comprehended by the inner spirit of man; it is an affair of commitment (*affectibus*) rather than of syllogisms, of life itself rather than disputation, of inspiration rather than learning, of conversion rather than reason" (p. 27).

6. Modern students are often surprised to find that "morality"—meaning the ritual observance of good conduct without the inner motivation of faith and love—is sometimes a bad word in seventeenth- and eighteenth-century texts. The condemnation, in *The Pilgrim's Progress,* of Mr. Legality, who dwells in the village of Morality, should be pondered. Sir John Hawkins says that he has treated of Johnson's religious life in considerable detail in order "to refute the objections of many infidels, who, desirous of having him thought to be of their party, endeavoured to make it believed, that he was a *mere moralist*" (B. H. Davis, ed., *The Life of Samuel Johnson, LL.D.* [New York: Macmillan, 1961], p. 246; my italics). But Johnson makes his position quite clear in his Sermon XIII: some men "please themselves with a constant regularity of life, and decency of behaviour. . . . Some are punctual in the attendance on public worship, and perhaps in the performance of private devotion. . . . Their religion is sincere; what is reprehensible is that it is partial, that the

heart is not yet purified" *(Works* [1825], IX, pp. 408–410). All thoughtful Christians of the time knew their *Epistle to the Romans,* and no modern student should attempt to expound their religious position without digesting it.

7. This axiom is also central to the post-Freudian psychiatry of Karen Horney and Erich Fromm and (one gathers) to Zen Buddhism and other non-Christian moral systems.

8. What Lionel Trilling has said of the modern novel ("Manners, Morals, and the Modern Novel," in *The Liberal Imagination* [New York: Viking, 1950], p. 222) as "the most effective agent of the moral imagination in our time"—"Its greatness and its practical usefulness [lies] in its unremitting work of involving the reader himself in the moral life, inviting him to put his own motives under examination, suggesting that reality is not as his conventional education has led him to see it"—will not surprise us if we consider its origins in the work of Bunyan and Defoe, Richardson, Fielding, and Sterne. Indeed, if there is any dominant motive in serious contemporary literature, it is surely the same contempt and rejection of the soul-destroying and ego-centered values of society— the socially inculcated concerns for money making, status seeking, image creating, power grabbing, ego gratification as the chief ends of life—that is found in dominant moral tradition in eighteenth-century English literature.

9. *Certain Sermons or Homilies Appointed by the King's Majesty to be Declared and Read by All Parsons, Vicars, and Curates, Every Sunday in Their Churches Where They Have Cure:* The Second Homily, "Of Faith" (probably by Cranmer).

10. *Ninety-Six Sermons* (Oxford: Parker, 1841), V, pp. 301, 308.

11. *Thirty-One Sermons* (Oxford: Parker, 1849), I, pp. 309–310.

12. *Sermons Preached upon Several Occasions* (London, 1737), I, pp. 68, 71.

13. *Works* (Oxford: Parker, 1847), II, p. 226.

14. For the orthodox Christian, of course, another source is revelation.

15. "All men are mortal; Socrates is a man; therefore Socrates is mortal." But, argues Mill, this conclusion, the product of the reasoning process allegedly unique to man, gives us no *new* knowledge: the fact was already known to us when we stated the major premise, *"All* men are mortal." Bertrand Russell amusingly illustrates the two kinds of epistemology: Aristotle, he says, by closing his eyes and cogitating, was able to deduce from the major premise that females are inferior to males, that women have fewer teeth than men. All Aristotle needed to do to verify this, Russell points out, was to ask Mrs. Aristotle to open her mouth for a few moments while he counted. But such a menial operation was beneath the dignity of rational man. This is perhaps unfair to Aristotle, who had a good deal of the empiricist spirit about him. Yet Sir Thomas Browne, in the wake of the Baconian revolution, properly derides Aristotle for asserting that "a man doth cough, but not an ox or cow; whereas the contrary is often observed by husbandman"; also that horses, oxen, and asses have no "eructation or belching" and that "man alone hath gray hairs" *(Vulgar Errors* [1646], Chap. VI).

16. The word "reason" of course has many meanings. Johnson's *Dictionary* (1755) distinguishes eleven, the first of which, "The power by which man deduces one proposition from another, or proceeds from premises to consequences," is the one intended in this sentence and generally in this chapter. But the other ten range through a wide spectrum of popular usage; and "reasonable," in the eighteenth as in other centuries, very often means no more than "appropriate, admirable, approved of by the speaker."

17. The popularizers of Baconianism were legion—Thomas Browne, Joseph Glanvill, Bishop Sprat, among others. One of the great popularizers of Locke was the Reverend Isaac Watts, whose life Johnson insisted be included in his *Lives of the Poets,* and to whom he pays the tribute, "Few books have been perused by me with greater pleasure than his *Improvement of the Mind,* of which the radical principles may indeed be found in Locke's *Conduct of the Understanding;* . . . Whoever has the care of instructing others may be charged with deficience in his duty if this book is not recommended" (*Life of Watts,* 1781).

18. *The Advancement of Learning,* in Sidney Warhaft, ed., *Francis Bacon, A Selection of His Works* (Toronto: Macmillan, 1965), p. 225; *The New Organon, ibid.,* p. 360. Cf. Christopher Hill, *Intellectual Origins of the English Revolution* (New York: Oxford University Press, 1965), p. 93: "It is important to realize that this religious element in early Baconianism was genuine. . . . Bacon professed no such narrow utilitarianism as later went under his name. In this respect he was as little a Baconian as Karl Marx was a Marxist."

19. *"La querelle des Anciens et Modernes"* began with the publication in France in the 1680's of works by Charles Perrault and Fontenelle complimenting the age of Louis XIV on its superiority in art, literature, and science over the relative crudeness of the Greeks and Romans. Boileau, Racine, and others properly rebutted this self-congratulation. Sir William Temple initiated the controversy in England by his *Essay upon the Ancient and Modern Learning* (1690), in which he takes an extravagantly anti-Modern position: everything has deteriorated since classical times; even in such minor genres as the fable and letter writing, the best practitioners were the early Greeks, Aesop and Phalaris. This "rediscovery" of the legendary Phalaris inspired the young Oxford scholar, Charles Boyle (with considerable unacknowledged assistance by senior classical scholars at Oxford), to publish an edition of "his" letters. This edition, in turn, was torn to pieces in a superb *Dissertation* (1699) by the great Richard Bentley of Cambridge, the foremost English classical scholar of all time. Bentley had no trouble in demonstrating that the works attributed to Aesop and Phalaris, far from being ancient, were very late Greek, and that Boyle and his helpers were very ignorant of what they professed to expertise in. Swift intervened in defense of his patron Temple with *The Battle of the Books* (1697; published 1704), satirizing Bentley's pugnacious temperament and his cousin Dryden's conceit as illustrations of Modern arrogance.

Though the implications of the *querelle* are worth examining—among other things, there were strong political overtones, Oxford being Tory and Cambridge Whig—the importance of the incident in the general history of ideas has perhaps been exaggerated by modern scholars. The complacent believer in the superiority of his own time is not unique to the seventeenth century, nor is the uncritical worshiper of the past, like Temple. Perrault's and Temple's essays are very trivial stuff, and even *The Battle of the Books,* charming as it is, is more of a *jeu d'esprit* than a serious treatment of the question; indeed, much of the humor of the piece comes from the devastating burlesque of the epic clichés of the Ancients, whose literary prowess Swift is supposed to be defending.

20. *History of the Royal Society* (1667), pp. 345, 366–367.

21. Preface to *A Dictionary of the English Language,* 1755. Robert South preached a series of sermons on "The fatal influence of words and names falsely applied," in which he says, "The generality of mankind is wholly and absolutely governed by words and names. . . . The multitude, or common rout, like a drove of sheep, or an herd of oxen, may be managed by any noise, or cry, which their drivers shall accustom them to. . . . They suffer themselves to be carried away with these puffs of wind, even contrary to knowledge and experience itself" (*Sermons Preached upon Several Occasions* [London, 1737], II, p. 33).

22. *Three Dialogues Between Hylas and Philonous,* beginning of the second dialogue. The profound seriousness and importance of Berkeley's epistemology has seldom been appreciated. Any reader who has an inclination to dismiss it with a smile should study A. A. Luce's short and readable analysis, *Berkeley's Immaterialism* (Edinburgh: Nelson, 1945).

23. *Philosophical Commentaries,* No. 769, in Berkeley, *Works,* ed. A. A. Luce and T. E. Jessup (Edinburgh: Nelson, 1948), I. If the basis of existentialism is, as we are told, the doctrine that "existence is prior to essence," it is hard to see what distinguishes it from philosophical empiricism. The teachings of Kierkegaard, with his fervent Augustinianism and violent anti-Hegelianism, deserve to be considered in connection with Swift and Johnson as much as with, say, Kafka and Sartre. Born in 1813, he is closer in time to the eighteenth century than to the twentieth.

24. Discussed in detail in Leslie Stephen's *English Thought in the Eighteenth Century* (1881)—a misnomer, since Stephen, a militant agnostic, is concerned chiefly to describe the deviations from orthodoxy.

25. The woolly and incoherent philosophical writings of the one-time political leader, Henry St. John, Lord Bolingbroke, have a somewhat similar Deist tendency. But they were little read by the general public, and were supposed (probably erroneously) to have made an impact by their assimilation by Pope in *An Essay on Man.*

26. The passage in *Rasselas* seems also to be satirizing the teaching of the Reverend Samuel Clarke, perhaps the one true rationalist of eighteenth-century English thought—Pope's "gloomy Clerk," who "took the high priori road,/And reasoned downward till we doubt of God." Clarke's Boyle Lectures (*A Discourse Concerning the Being and Attributes of God,* delivered 1704–1705), in which he proves the existence of God, and many other things, in a strictly logical, or mathematical, series of theorems, are an amazing performance. "The fitness arising from the relations and qualities of causes and effects," one of the phrases of the philosopher in *Rasselas,* is Clarkean terminology, though Clarke inherits it from the general Stoic tradition.

27. It may be noted that the practice of capitalizing pronouns referring to the Deity is nineteenth-century usage, not earlier. Serious theological writing in the twentieth century seems to have abandoned it.

28. A. O. Lovejoy, *The Great Chain of Being* (Cambridge, Mass.: Harvard University Press, 1936). Because of the popularity of Lovejoy's book, students sometimes tend to assume that everyone in the eighteenth century must have believed in the existence of the "great chain." This is not so. Johnson's devastating attack on the concept will be noted; and it is hard, apart from King, Pope, and Soame Jenyns, to find extended discussions of it in eighteenth-century English writing. Thomson and Addison refer to it; perhaps traces of "chain of being" thinking can be detected in Burke; but on the whole the century was certainly not under its spell.

29. *The Life of Samuel Johnson LL.D.,* September 23, 1777.

30. When, late in the century, the younger Pitt, a student of Adam Smith, initiated the policy of government withdrawal from economic intervention that was to become the rule in nineteenth-century Britain, the Secretary of the Treasury of the young United States, Alexander Hamilton, enunciated (in his *Report on Manufactures*) and initiated the opposite policy of close protection of American industry by means of import tariffs imposed by the federal government. To what extent the subsequent economic histories of the two countries is evidence of the ultimate wisdom of either theory is a complex question; but in 1929 Britain formally abandoned free trade, and has shown no signs of wanting to return to it.

31. Review of Robert Southey, *Sir Thomas More; or Colloquies on the Progress and Prospects of Society.*

32. A version of part of this chapter appeared as an article, "Augustinianism and Empiricism," in *Eighteenth-Century Studies,* I (Fall 1967), 33–68.

Four

The Arts

General Chronology: Some Dates in the History of the Arts and Aesthetics

1660   Theaters reopened in London (under royal patronage), after the Puritan ban in 1641.

1660's and 1670's. Sir Peter Lely (born and trained in Holland) active; painted luscious portraits of the ladies of Charles II's court.

1666   The Great Fire destroys much of the old City of London, including the old Gothic St. Paul's cathedral. Sir Christopher Wren commissioned to redesign the City (though his plans were not carried out). But his many baroque City churches and his great baroque St. Paul's (built 1675 to 1710) were erected.

1671   Grinling Gibbons, woodcarver, discovered in Holland by John Evelyn, and brought to England; carved woodwork for Wren's St. Paul's and new London churches.

1675   Godfrey Kneller, later Sir Godfrey, Bart., born in Germany and trained in Holland, arrives in England. Leading portraitist of next four decades. Noted for his set of portraits of the Kit-Cat Club, leading Whig politicians and intellectuals, like Addison and Steele.

1680   Caius Gabriel Cibber, statues of Madness at gates of Bethlehem Hospital (Bedlam).

1680's and 1690's. Henry Purcell active. Organist of Westminster Abbey and the Chapel Royal. His opera *Dido and Aeneas,* 1689.

1699   Castle Howard designed by Sir John Vanbrugh and Nicholas Hawksmoor (completed 1710); Blenheim Palace designed 1705, completed 1724.

1708   William Croft, organist of Westminster Abbey.

1710   George Frederick Handel comes to England; his opera *Rinaldo,* 1711, stirs up controversy. Naturalized a British subject 1726.

1711   Parliamentary act subsidizing building of fifty new metropolitan churches (only a few actually built).

1716   Burlington House rebuilt by the third Earl of Burlington and Colin Campbell in Palladian style. Burlington later becomes patron of William Kent.

1718   Maurice Greene appointed organist of St. Paul's.

1718–   Handel director of music to the Duke of Chandos at Canons.
20

1726   James Gibbs, St. Martin's-in-the-Fields.

1728   John Gay, *The Beggar's Opera.*

1732   Vauxhall pleasure gardens under management of Jonathan Tyers.

1733   Thomas Arne, music for Addison's opera *Rosamund.*

1735   William Hogarth, "The Rake's Progress."

1740   Thomas Arne, music for James Thomson's masque, *Alfred* (includes "Rule Britannia").

1740's and later. Lancelot ("Capability") Brown active in landscape gardening; designs the gardens at Blenheim and Kew.

1742   Handel, *Messiah* first performed (in Dublin); Ranelagh gardens opened.

1747   Horace Walpole begins Gothic additions to Strawberry Hill.

1750's to 1770's. Richard Wilson active in landscape painting.

1750's to 1780's. Thomas Gainsborough active in portrait and landscape painting.

1750's to 1790's. Sir Joshua Reynolds active in portrait painting.

1754   Thomas Chippendale, *The Gentleman and Cabinet Maker's Director.*

1753   Hogarth's aesthetic treatise, *The Analysis of Beauty.*

1755   William Boyce, master of the King's band of musicians.

1756   Edmund Burke, *A Philosophical Inquiry into the Origin of Our Ideas of the Sublime and Beautiful.*

1757   Sir William Chambers, *Designs of Chinese Buildings, Furniture, etc.;* beginning of "chinoiserie" in architecture and interior decoration.
       Robert Adam, *The Ruins of the Palace of Diocletian.*

1760's to 1790's. Joseph Nollekens active in statuary.

1762   Johann Christian Bach (eleventh son of Johann Sebastian) settles in England.
       Henry Home, Lord Kames, *Elements of Criticism;* James ("Athenian") Stuart, *The Antiquities of Athens.*

1762–   Horace Walpole, *Anecdotes of Painting in England,* based on
71   the collections of George Vertue.

1764   Mozart (aged eight) visits England; performs before royal family.

1768   Royal Academy of Arts founded; Reynolds first president, Gainsborough, Wilson, and most other eminent artists of the time members.

1775   Sir William Chambers, Somerset House.

1776   Sir John Hawkins, *General History of Music;* Charles Burney, *History of Music* (to 1789).

1784   First Handel festival, in Westminster Abbey.

1790   Archibald Alison, *Essay on the Nature and Principles of Taste*.

1791   Franz Josef Haydn's first visit to England; his "London" symphonies performed; awarded Doctor of Music degree by Oxford.

Introductory: The Baroque

As many have complained, the word "baroque" has come to be used as loosely, and is as impossible of strict definition, as, say, "Romantic." Its original signification seems to have been "bizarre, *outré*, barbaric," which, interestingly, is exactly what "Gothic" and its cognate "grotesque" originally meant as descriptions of art. Yet it is meaningful to say that the dominant artistic idiom of Restoration and eighteenth-century Britain is essentially that of the baroque and its child, the rococo. Perhaps as good a definition of baroque as any is the use of exuberant ornamentation on a carefully planned, symmetrical base; rococo is a more delicate version of the same. They are *dramatic* performances, rejoicing in bright colors, exaggeration, startling contrast, overpowering the spectator or auditor with sheer energy and diversity. One thinks of Handel's great choruses, Vanbrugh's Blenheim Palace, Reynolds' more florid portraits, the portrait sculpture of Roubiliac and Nollekens, Chippendale's furniture (especially of the "Chinese" variety), and, to pick some literary examples in various genres, Dryden's *Ode on the Death of Mrs. Anne Killigrew,* Congreve's *The Way of the World,* the fourth book of Pope's *The Dunciad,* Sterne's *Tristram Shandy*.

To the nineteenth century, all this kind of thing was anath-

ema: it connoted frivolity, lack of "high seriousness," artificiality
—as though all art were not, by definition, artificial!—deca-
dence, and general immorality. Ruskin becomes almost hysteri-
cal as he denounces the moral degeneracy of baroque architecture, and the respected historian John Richard Green sums it
up in a sentence of almost incredible self-righteousness: "We
instinctively feel the great, the immeasurable distance that severs
this age [he is writing in 1859], so proud of its truth, its earnest-
ness, its energy, its high and noble aims, from the heartlessness,
the indifference, the frivolity—in one word, the utter world-
liness of the eighteenth century." [1]

Only fairly recently has the image created by the neurotic
blindness of the Victorians to this great period of art started to
disappear. It first began to do so in music: it became harder and
harder to accuse Bach's great B-minor mass, supremely baroque
as it is, of frivolity and "lack of depth," though one still occasionally finds the older person who carries on the Victorian tradition of accusing Bach's music of "arid, mathematical rationality." Most North Americans are still a little suspicious of the
splendor of Wren's St. Paul's Cathedral, gleaming in white and
gold, and feel the "dim, religious light" of Victorian pseudo-
Gothic churches somehow more "moral." Why bright light and
splendor should be thought irreligious is hard to say, considering that light has always been the prime symbol of deity. But
more recent church architecture has gone back to the earlier
conception and is not afraid to let in plenty of light on religious
"mystery."

The use of "baroque" as a strict descriptive term in art criticism is probably of less value than the role it plays in reminding
the modern student that a whole continent of exciting aesthetic
experience may lie outside the boundaries of his limited education. Thus Evelyn Waugh (whose early training was as an artist)
makes the word symbolize the freeing of an Oxford undergraduate of the 1920's, the protagonist of his most intimately autobio-
graphical novel, *Brideshead Revisited,* from the cold, self-centered inhibition of his essentially Victorian upbringing. As an
adolescent, Charles Ryder says,

> . . . though in opinion I had made that easy leap, from the puri-
> tanism of Ruskin to the puritanism of Roger Fry, my sentiments at
> heart were insular and mediaeval.

His release is effected when he becomes acquainted with a great eighteenth-century English country house, Brideshead Castle:

> This was my conversion to the baroque. Here under that high and insolent dome, under those tricky ceilings; here, as I passed through those arches and broken pediments to the pillared shade beyond and sat, hour by hour, before the fountain, probing its shadows, tracing its lingering echoes, rejoicing in all its clustered feats of daring and invention, I felt a whole new system of nerves alive within me, as though the water that spurted and bubbled among its stones was indeed a life-giving spring.[2]

Many young Englishmen and Americans, on whom the dead hand of Ruskin, whether they know it or not, lies heavy even today, probably need to experience a similar "conversion" if they are really to appreciate the glories of English literature of the eighteenth century (and, indeed, the seventeenth as well). The dazzling ornamentation of Pope's poetry, the breath-taking power of Swift's wit, the elaborate grandeur of Johnson's prose —for that matter, the exotic diction and involuted sentences of Milton—have much in common with the coloratura and verve of Bach's and Handel's music, the sheer melodrama of Vanbrugh's and Hawksmoor's architecture (pushed to even further lengths in South German and Hispanic baroque), the extravagant curlicues of Grinling Gibbons's woodcarvings, the exuberance of line and color in a drawing room decorated by Adam or furnished by Chippendale or Sheraton.

Such a conversion is probably one from a state in which the chief response to an object of art is not aesthetic at all, but "social" or self-regarding—one "likes" a Victorian pseudo-Gothic church or a piece of sentimental Victorian poetry because one knows that this is the way churches ought to look and poetry ought to read, and the pleasure one gets from the experience is largely that of feeling pleased with oneself for doing the right thing—to a state in which one begins to react directly and vividly to the materials of art themselves, the sound, the line, the color, the imagery. As Waugh puts it, a new, or at least hitherto unused, system of nerves begins to operate. Eighteenth-century art is never derivative in the sense of seeking to get its effects by appealing to the observer's historical knowledge—as nineteenth-century art so frequently did. A writer in the eleventh edition of the *Encyclopaedia Britannica* contrasts them (rather unexpectedly, for this publication of 1910 often presents the ripest fruit of the Victorian sensibility),

> The 19th century is the period *par excellence* of architectural "re-vivals." The great Renaissance movement in Italy . . . was some-thing more than a mere revival. It was a new spirit affecting the whole of art and literature and life, not an architectural move-ment only; and as far as architecture is concerned it was not a mere imitative revival. The great Italian architects of the Renaissance, as well as Wren, Vanbrugh, and Hawksmoor in England, however they drew their inspiration from antique models, were for the most part original architects; they put the ancient materials to new uses of their own. The tendency of the 19th-century revivals, on the other hand, except in France, was distinctly imitative in a sense in which the architecture of the great Renaissance period was not. Correctness of imitation, in the English Gothic revival especially, was an avowed object; and conformity to precedent became, in fact, except with one or two individual architects, almost the admitted test of excellence.[3]

"Correctness of imitation" and "conformity to precedent" as avowed objects on the part of artists! It is exactly the charge Victorian critics were fond of making against eighteenth-century literature, and if it could be substantiated, it would be a damn-ing one. But of course it cannot be; there is nothing in earlier literature remotely like the great writings of Dryden, Pope, Swift, and Johnson, to name the most important figures. Like all great artists their genius is original, and they had no intention of merely duplicating what had been done before. In Victorian ar-chitecture, alas, the charge is only too easy to document. In many ways, important aspects of both Romanticism and Victorianism in England seem to represent a failure of nerve after the eight-eenth-century's full-blooded acceptance and extension of the Renaissance spirit of invention and exploration. Certainly few critics could now be found to deny that English painting, archi-tecture, and music in the nineteenth century constitute an inglorious decline from the brilliance of those arts in the eight-eenth.

As in other matters, what happened in English art in the sev-enteenth and eighteenth centuries was a cross-fertilization be-tween sturdy, independent, if provincial, native energy and the wider vision and technical expertise of the Continental tradition. This is well put in the opening paragraph of the volume of the Oxford History of Art series dealing with the seventeenth and early eighteenth centuries:

> The Stuart period is one of the richest and most absorbing in the history of the arts in England. The sheer quantity of works of art that were produced between the reigns of James I and George I was far greater than in the age of the Tudors and, though much of it would be deservedly neglected by a historian of European or even of English art, it contained some of the most vigorous and beautiful expressions of the English genius.

But this is only the prelude to full maturity:

> The flowering of that genius in the Hanoverian age grew partly out of a fusion in the earlier period of native and continental influences, and the English reaction to the full baroque style of the Continent is the central problem: a problem affected by growing consciousness of the arts, by rapidly increasing first-hand acquaintance with renaissance and modern art on the Continent and by varied trends in patronage, from the highly developed cosmopolitan tastes of some of the Stuart sovereigns and the aristocracy to the reactionary, or actively hostile, views of less sophisticated patrons.[4]

It need only be added that the first two Hanoverian monarchs were at least as cosmopolitan in taste as their Stuart ancestors—indeed, their cosmopolitanism was held against them by disaffected English oppositionists, who sneered at their patronage of Handel—and that George III did not extend the insularity of his political outlook to artistic matters, but gave his patronage to the Venetian Canaletto as well as to the native Gainsborough, and recognized no national boundaries in his encouragement of music. Continental painters from Lely and Kneller to Angelica Kauffmann and Henry Fuseli (following in the footsteps of Holbein, Rubens, and Van Dyck) came to practice their art in England and often found so receptive a clientele that they settled there.

For young English painters and architects, an extended visit to Italy, the home of their art, became almost a compulsory part of their education. Handel, a Saxon, spent three years maturing his art in Italy before moving to England. The tours of the Continent in 1770 and 1772 by Johnson's friend, the pioneer musicologist Charles Burney, and the volumes he published describing them, *The Present State of Music in France and Italy* and *The Present State of Music in Germany, the Netherlands, and the United Provinces,* are significant of the concern he felt that music in England should be regarded in an international, not merely a local, context, a concern which is also present in his monumental *History of Music,* as well as in its rival, Hawkins' *General History of Music.* The most noted sculptors of the time, Cibber, Rysbrack, Roubiliac, Scheemakers, were immigrants; one, the most popular and best of the latter part of the century, Nollekens, was the son of an immigrant painter. Singers, then as now, wandered over the world, and if some of Handel's most famous *prime donne* were imports, like the notorious rivals Faustina and Cuzzoni, he also found competent native singers, like Susanna Arne (Mrs. Theophilus Cibber), who first sang the great contralto solos in *Messiah;* and British singers in turn began to perform on the Continent, like Michael Kelly, who sang Basilio in the first performance of Mozart's *Nozze di Figaro.*

The question of the influence of the cosmopolitan spirit of the time on literature is, of course, a harder one, because of the necessarily isolating influence of the language in which it is written. Yet Dryden, Pope, and Johnson were properly insistent on the necessity of an acquaintance with serious Continental literatures, and, without in any way sacrificing their own originality, of recognizing that English literature, like the other arts, must be amenable to judgment by international, not merely insular, standards of excellence. Many writers, as well as painters and musicians, made a kind of extended Grand Tour of the Continent in their youth. Gibbon and Hume, Beckford and Horace Walpole and Boswell were genuine cosmopolitans, as much at home on the Continent as in Britain, almost as fluent in French as in English (Gibbon and Beckford both composed important works in French; Hume retired to France to write his masterpiece, *A Treatise of Human Nature*).

At the end of the century, the long ordeal of the French Revolutionary and Napoleonic wars, lasting over two decades—and, perhaps, the nationalistic and introvertive tendencies of Romanticism—again tended to isolate English writing. Not until the voices of T. S. Eliot and Ezra Pound were heard in the twentieth century did something like the eighteenth century's recognition of literature as a supranational art again exist, and it is questionable whether even yet in the twentieth century Eliot's and Pound's exhortations to a more than national outlook on literature have been much heeded in practice by the average writer and reader of English literature.

Music

English music of the late seventeenth and the eighteenth centuries has more continuity with its past than do the other arts of the time. The Continental influence began to be felt in the reign of Charles II, chiefly the influence of Italian monody—the emphasis on the solo with accompaniment—such as Monteverdi's, in displacing the older polyphonic tradition, and also perhaps some French influence, stemming from the operatic work of Lully, Louis XIV's court composer. But, as did not happen in painting and architecture, it encountered and merged with a thriving and vigorous native professional tradition.

Since early Tudor times, various musical organizations in Westminster and London had maintained high standards of performance and repertoire, notably the choir of the Chapel Royal and the royal band of musicians, maintained by the Court[5] and the choir and organists of Westminster Abbey, St. Paul's, and the larger churches of the metropolis. For some decades, musical societies commissioned and performed an ode on Saint Cecilia's Day, November 22, in honor of the patroness of music, which called forth some of the finest achievements of librettists (such as Dryden, Congreve, and Pope), composers (both Purcell and Handel), and performers. The composition of a setting of the Poet Laureate's annual Birthday Ode and New Year's Ode in honor of the sovereign, and its performance at Court on the stated day, at least gave employment and practice to composers, singers, and instrumentalists, even though the poetic texts were notorious for their badness and not much of the music seems to have been inspired (though Handel's setting of Nahum Tate's ode for Queen Anne's birthday in 1713 has been given a modern recording). Coronations, royal funerals and returns from abroad, military victories and peace treaties called for public ceremonies for which fine music was written by the best composers available.

To serve these institutions and occasions there existed a closely knit community of singers, instrumentalists, and composers—all three functions sometimes united in a single individual —perpetuating itself by training youngsters (often their own children) as apprentices and eventually successors. Thus there was a continuity of tradition from Taverner, in Henry VII's reign, through Byrd in Elizabeth's and Lawes in Charles I's, to Purcell in the reigns of the later Stuarts and Handel in those of the early Hanoverians.[6] As well as this great musical center in London, the college chapels at Oxford and Cambridge and the provincial cathedrals also often maintained fine choirs—those of the two Protestant cathedrals in Dublin combined for the first performance of Handel's *Messiah* and no doubt had much to do with forming and sustaining the fine musical tradition of that city which persisted to the time of Shaw and Joyce, and beyond. Occasionally, enlightened and wealthy noblemen—Milton's Earl of Bridgewater, Pope's Earl of Burlington and Duke of Chandos—had their domestic musicians and musical directors, that of Chandos no less than Handel himself. Throughout the century, one of the regular attractions of the immensely popular public pleasure gardens of Ranelagh and Vauxhall was what would now be called "pop concerts," at which the most notable singers, orchestras, and conductors performed—even Handel participated—while the audience strolled, ate, and drank.

The rich musical fare provided during the period of the Restoration and the eighteenth century did not lack appreciative auditors. Much has been written about the musical versatility and taste of the average Elizabethan gentleman. Not much formal study of the question seems to have been made, but certainly amateurs of music abounded in the seventeenth and eighteenth centuries. Pepys' constant delight in music is one of the most striking features of his wonderful *Diary:* few days pass when the hard-working, efficient civil servant cannot find time to practice on his viol, sing part-songs with his friends, criticize some new singer or composition, even compose songs of his own. All of the eminent North family were musical; its head, Lord Guilford, told Evelyn that he had been brought up from childhood to read music at sight, and another member, Roger North, wrote pioneering treatises of musicology and music criticism. Garrett Wesley or Wellesley, Earl of Mornington, distant cousin of John and Charles Wesley and father of the great Duke of Wellington, the Marquess Wellesley, and other distinguished sons, was Doctor and Professor of Music in Trinity College, Dublin, and a respectable composer. Many portraits of families engaged in making music exist, notably that by the elder Nollekens of Frederick, Prince of Wales, as a boy, playing the cello in company with his sisters the Princesses, who are playing the lute and harpsichord and singing (it was these Princesses, George II's daughters, for whom Handel wrote much of his keyboard music by way of supplying them with lesson material). Late in the century, the young ladies of Jane Austen's novels are expected, as a matter of course, to sing and to perform on "the instrument," as she amusingly calls it—the new pianoforte, which was replacing the harpsichord—and, as Mary Bennet's father acidly puts it, "delight" the guests of the family.

With the great Handel commemoration of 1784, the first music festival in history designed to honor a composer, and with the inauguration of the annual Three Choirs festival, those of the cathedrals of Worcester, Gloucester, and Hereford, the taste for oratorio singing, still widespread in the English-speaking world, began to flourish. George III patronized both activities, and even Samuel Johnson, notoriously unsusceptible to music—though he did once admit to being fond of "Let Ambition Fire Thy Mind"—condescended to write the noble dedication to the King of Charles Burney's official account of the Handel commemoration. It was an Englishman, Samuel Wesley, son of Charles, the poet, and nephew of the great John, who discovered and first publicized to the world at large the achievement of the obscure Johann Sebastian Bach.

It was the great age of "catch" clubs and glee societies. More "popular" music that is still current probably comes from the eighteenth century than from any other. The traditional patriotic songs of the English-speaking world are of that period—

"God Save the King" (alias "America"), "Rule Britannia" (music by Thomas Arne), "Heart of Oak" (music by William Boyce), "Men of Harlech," "Scots Wha Hae," "The Minstrel Boy" and other tunes of Moore's *Irish Melodies,* the tune of "The Star-Spangled Banner." So are many of the most familiar (and best) hymn tunes—even "Adeste, Fideles," which most people think of as vaguely medieval, but which is a perfectly typical eighteenth-century song. So are most of the traditional repertoire of country dance tunes, such as "Sir Roger de Coverley," after whom Addison named his hero (the dance and the tune are better known in America as "the Virginia Reel"). There was never a period that had a greater flair for a catchy melody. Many of the best of them are collected in the six volumes of Tom Durfey's popular *Pills to Purge Melancholy,* the last of the many recensions of which he published in 1720—Addison tells us (in *Guardian* 67) that he remembered seeing Charles II leaning familiarly on Durfey's shoulder and humming a song along with him—and were immortalized in Gay's *The Beggar's Opera.*

The period is dominated by two of the greatest names in the history of music, Henry Purcell, who lived during the reigns of Charles II, James II, and William III, and George Frederick Handel, who served the courts of Anne, George I, and George II. The work of each is a large subject for study in itself; few musicologists, not to mention mere amateurs of music, are thoroughly familiar with the extensive *oeuvre* of either (it has been estimated that the total "output" of Handel equals that of Beethoven and Bach combined). Most of it is extant, and each year more and more neglected masterpieces by both are being resuscitated and performed to the delight of listeners.

Purcell was the son of a court musician, a tenor singer of the Chapel Royal, and later successor in the royal "private music" to Milton's friend, Henry Lawes; his uncle was master of the choristers of Westminster Abbey. Henry was enrolled as a chorister of the Chapel Royal, perhaps as early as the age of six, and during the rest of his life he was occupied in some official post or other in the musical organizations of the capital, succeeding his teacher Dr. John Blow as organist of Westminster Abbey at the age of twenty. He was thus responsible for the music at the coronations of James II and William and Mary. His official duties produced birthday odes and songs of welcome for Charles II, James II, Queen Mary II, and the little Duke of Gloucester, Queen Anne's last surviving child. Most impressive, perhaps, of all these compositions is the great funeral anthem for Queen Mary in 1694, "Thou knowest, Lord, the secrets of our hearts." His *Te Deum* and *Jubilate,* composed for the St. Cecilia's Day celebration of 1694, continued to be performed annually at St. Paul's, and later alternately with Handel's *Te Deum* and *Jubilate* for the Peace of Utrecht. But many other examples of his church music—anthems, settings of psalms and canticles and of the Anglican services—survive and deserve being performed.

The work of Purcell's most widely known today is his opera *Dido and Aeneas,* with libretto by Nahum Tate. Fine as it is, it is only a small sampling of his dramatic music; he wrote five other operas, including versions of two plays by Dryden, two by Shakespeare, and one by Beaumont and Fletcher, and incidental music, including well over a hundred songs, for forty-three other plays (the high musical content of Restoration drama is often forgotten by students), dozens of other songs and catches, and a respectable amount of excellent instrumental music.

Critics have always found it hard to agree on a neat assessment of Purcell's achievement, except that it is that of a rare and authentic genius (though certainly not a neglected one—both he and Handel received an immense amount of acclaim from their contemporaries). Perhaps the best is the saying that Purcell is "not for timid souls." Much has been made of the assertion that he was the last genuinely English composer, and lamentations used to be heard that the triumphs of the "foreigner" Handel had given "native" music, as represented by Purcell, its quietus. Great music is not so easily nationalized as this; what the statement probably means is simply that Purcell, raised in the school of Byrd and Lawes, was still in the process of turning from the older polyphonic to the newer monodic tradition. But like all real artists he was glad to learn what he could from other masters of his trade, such as the Italian Corelli and the Frenchman Lully.

Contrariwise, lamentations have been heard that he did not make this transition cleanly enough: Sir Donald Tovey goes so

far as to talk of "the almost tragic blending of genius and failure" in the English church music of the Restoration, and of the
"patchiness" of Purcell's work, maintaining that he "is probably
the only instance in music of a man of really high genius born
out of due time." Such teleological approaches seem beside the
point to those who are willing simply to obtain delight from the
technical brilliance and emotional depth of *Dido and Aeneas,*
the *Te Deum,* and the funeral anthem for Queen Mary, and
the enduring charm of the songs and incidental music to the
plays. Purcell's musical voice *is* idiosyncratic; he has his own
unique and unmistakable idiom. This makes him exasperating
for critics who would like to pigeonhole him neatly, but it no
more prejudices the excellence of his music than a similar
uniqueness prejudices the excellence of the poetry of Purcell's
great admirer, Gerard Manley Hopkins, who wrote of him that
"he has . . . uttered in notes the very make and species of man
as created both in him and in all men generally," and of his
music,

> . . . so some great stormfowl, whenever he has walked his while
> The thunder-purple seabeach plumèd purple-of-thunder,
> If a wuthering of his palmy snow-pinions scatter a colossal smile
> Off him, but meaning motion fans fresh our wits with wonder.

Purcell was great; but Handel, one of the supreme musical
giants of all time, transcends classification. Haydn said of the
oratorio *Joshua* that he "was perfectly certain that only one inspired author ever did, or ever could, pen so sublime a composition." Mozart painstakingly reorchestrated *Messiah, Acis and
Galatea,* and the settings of Dryden's two St. Cecilia's Day odes
for modern orchestra. Beethoven said of him, "He was the greatest composer that ever lived. I would uncover my head and
kneel before his tomb." Bach, then an obscure provincial organist, painfully trudged some twenty-five miles hoping to get a
glimpse of his world-famous contemporary, who was back in his
native town of Halle for a short visit, only to miss him and
trudge back again.

An infant prodigy like Mozart (but, unlike him, without paternal encouragement), Handel early learned the harpsichord,
organ, violin, and oboe; the last instrument was his early love,

and to judge from his use of it in his compositions, always a favorite; but it was on the keyboard instruments that he—unusually for a great composer—became the greatest virtuoso performer of his time. He had a better academic education than most composers of his age—he attended the University of Halle for a time—and a sound musical education in the fine idiom of church music of Schütz and Buxtehude. In his late teens Handel nearly succeeded Buxtehude as organist as Lübeck, but declined the post when he learned that the offer entailed his marrying Buxtehude's elderly daughter (he remained a bachelor all his life). Between the ages of twenty-one and twenty-four he lived in Italy, where he was lionized by the Italian musical community; more than with any other composer, the cross-fertilization of northern and Mediterranean culture bore rich fruit in Handel's music.

Well aware of his capabilities and determined to realize them, Handel accepted from the Elector Georg Ludwig the splendid appointment of musical director to the Hanoverian court, only to absent himself, with or without permission, for the even richer opportunities of London. When Queen Anne died, the Elector, now King George I, and Handel were reunited (it is a pity that the charming story of Handel's regaining George's good graces by composing the lovely *Water Music* has turned out to be a myth). For the next half century he bestrode English music like a colossus; indeed, even longer, for George III, only twenty-one when Handel died, worshiped him even more fervently than his predecessors had done, and helped to institute the cult of Handel which still flourishes enthusiastically among English (and American) amateurs of choral music.

Handel wrote fifty operas, twenty oratorios, a hundred cantatas and "serenatas," fifty concerti for various instruments (including the eighteen wonderful *concerti grossi* and the seventeen organ concerti), some thirty anthems, two (early) Passions, much solo music for harpsichord, violin, flute, and oboe, and incidental music to a few plays. The operas, marvels of composition which seem to explore the whole potential of the human voice, used to be sneered at because of their lack of dramatic action. But the drama of Handel is in his music; few aspects of human tragedy, comedy, fear, pathos, awe, rejoicing are left un-

expressed in the operas, more and more of which are being revived and performed as twentieth-century audiences discover
their glories. Most of the oratorios were kept alive during the
nineteenth century by English amateur choirs, often of work-
men in the industrial districts of the North, who would not be
deterred by the objections of Victorian critics to what they
thought to be Handel's lack of romanticism. But some of these
oratorios still deserve to be better known than they are.

The instrumental music, to judge from mid-twentieth-century
record catalogues, is beginning to be done justice to; so is the
fine ceremonial music for public occasions, the Coronation Anthems and the fine *Te Deums* for the Peace of Utrecht and the
victory of Dettingen (one can imagine the piercing trumpets
and thundering kettledrums resounding among the white-and-
gold baroque glories of Wren's St. Paul's, as the monarch and
his court, resplendent in their ceremonial robes, give thanks on
behalf of the nation), the lovely *Water Music,* the impressive
music for the Royal Fireworks celebrating the Peace of Aix-la-
Chapelle. For the last, since it was an outdoor occasion, Handel
introduced twenty-four oboes, twelve bassoons, nine trumpets,
nine horns, three pairs of kettledrums, and no less than 101 can-
non, of various calibres, equivalent to several regiments of artil-
lery. After that, no one can continue to talk of the eighteenth
century's restraint—Tchaikowsky is hopelessly outclassed.

It is useless to argue that Handel is not the greatest *English*
composer. English monarchs, since his time, have been regularly
crowned and buried to Handel's music ("Zadok the Priest" and
the Dead March in *Saul*); and a sizable number of George II's
many sins should be forgiven him for the occasion on which the
irascible little monarch, irresistibly moved by the sound, rose to
his feet when he first heard the Hallelujah Chorus in *Messiah,*
since when—for no one should remain seated when a king
stands—all subsequent audiences have followed his example.
The Germans, seeking to adopt Handel as they have adopted
Shakespeare, often translate the English words of his oratorios
back into his native German; but Handel in German merely
sounds silly.

Students of literature should be particularly interested in
Handel's settings of English poetry, which often provide a won-

derfully intelligent and sensitive commentary on the poetic text. The best known are those of Dryden's two great St. Cecilia's Day odes, which superseded settings by earlier musicians. Handel's reinforcement of Dryden's attempt, in the earlier ode, to characterize the contrasting "passions" roused by music is brilliant, and the concluding "last trumpet" passage is breathtaking—a single, unaccompanied soprano voice sings a steeply ascending broken chord, presently joined, on a prolonged high note, by a single trumpet; and, when it seems that the note cannot possibly be sustained any longer, the entire chorus and orchestra suddenly come crashing in like a gigantic thunder stroke, as of worlds breaking asunder, and continue fortissimo with a monumental and intricate fugue on the words "The dead shall live, the living die, And music shall untune the sky," as though Handel, with consummate audacity, were actually trying to reproduce the music of that untuning.

Handel's settings of the words of the King James Bible, in *Messiah* and other oratorios, do justice to its magnificent poetry. Milton's *L'Allegro* and *Il Penseroso* are perfect material for Handelian tone painting (at which Handel is at least as adept as Richard Strauss). The best introduction for the beginner to the exquisiteness of Pope's poetry is Handel's setting of two couplets from the pastoral "Summer" inserted in the masque *Semele* (libretto by Congreve):

> Where'er you walk, cool gales shall fan the glade;
> Trees, where you sit, shall crowd into a shade;
> Where'er you tread, the blushing flow'rs shall rise,
> And all things flourish, where'er you turn your eyes.

Few could tamper with Pope's versification without disaster; but Handel's change of Pope's "where" in the last line to "where'er," necessitated by the music, does not make it worse. Finest of all, perhaps, is the setting of Gay's *Acis and Galatea,* the quintessence of modern pastoral—both Gay and Handel at their most subtly sophisticated. That Gay and Handel achieved this magnificently successful collaboration seems to discount the assertion, encountered so frequently in literary histories, that *The Beggar's Opera* expressed Gay's dislike of Italian (Handelian) opera and indeed succeeded in extinguishing it. *The Beg-*

gar's Opera is a masterpiece of drama, and Gay's handling of the folk tunes he uses in it is masterly, their charming simplicity adding another level to the already complex texture of irony in the piece. But it is certainly not a serious contribution to *musical* art.

These two great names, Handel and Purcell, tend to eclipse the rest; yet besides them the Restoration period and the eighteenth century produced a group of native musicians as respectable, to say the least, as their counterparts in the nineteenth century. Among them were holders of appointments in the cathedrals and at the Court, at Oxford and Cambridge, compilers of useful musicological treatises, composers whose music, on the comparatively rare occasions it is now heard, gives genuine pleasure; and, thanks to modern recordings, the occasions are becoming less rare. Some of them are Jeremiah Clarke (whose extremely popular "Trumpet Voluntary" has often been attributed to Purcell); William Croft and Maurice Greene, editors of a fine collection of English church music; William Boyce, master of the royal band and composer of charming orchestral symphonies. The music of these men is sometimes heard without the authorship being recognized, often in the way of familiar hymn tunes—"St. Anne's," the noble tune of Isaac Watts's noble hymn "O God, our help in ages past," is by Croft; so is "Hanover" ("O worship the King all glorious above")—and "traditional" songs, like Boyce's lively setting of Garrick's tribute to the *annus mirabilis* 1759, "Come, cheer up, my lads, 'tis to glory we steer,/ To add something new to this wonderful year. . . . Heart of oak are our ships,/ Jolly tars are our men. . . ."

Best known, and probably best, of these lesser composers is Thomas Augustine Arne, "Doctor Arne" after Oxford conferred its Doctor of Music degree on him. (Handel had indignantly refused the offer of such a degree, it was said, when he learned that the honor would cost him some £5 in registration fees. But later in the century the university redeemed itself by bestowing one on Haydn, *gratis* one hopes.) Arne was a prolific composer of successful light opera, settings of operas and masques by Addison, Fielding, Congreve, and others, and incidental music to plays, notably Shakespeare's. His settings of Shakespearean songs—"Where the Bee Sucks," "When Daisies Pied," "Under the Greenwood Tree," "Blow, Blow, Thou Winter Wind"—are still almost the standard settings, and are indeed praiseworthy attempts to capture something of the Elizabethan spirit in baroque idiom. The soprano arias in his serious opera *Artaxerxes* were for a long time part of the standard coloratura repertoire and are happily beginning to be heard again.

Architecture, Interior Decorating, Landscape Gardening

Georgian architecture is one of the glories of the English past. Economically speaking, it was, like other things in the eighteenth century, a by-product of an expanding and affluent individualistic society. As has happened in all times and places, when men have grown wealthy they have invested their wealth in more lavish buildings and furnishings; and from the reign of Elizabeth through that of Victoria, England experienced a more or less continuous building boom. "Housing developments" in the cities, especially London, were undertaken on a speculative basis then as now. Sometimes (as now) they were unsuccessful— the investor lost his money, or the result was a set of jerry-built houses that rapidly fell to pieces; when Samuel Johnson wrote in his poem *London,* 1738, that "falling houses thunder on your head," he was not merely using poetic license.

When sound financing and architectural finesse were combined, however, as often happened in the later seventeenth and eighteenth centuries, the result was the noble series of "squares," still one of the finest features of London. These squares were named after the aristocratic families who had (usually) inherited the land and astutely invested their capital in the buildings—Berkeley Square, Grosvenor Square, Manchester Square; the Russells' Bedford Square, Bloomsbury Square, Russell Square, Tavistock Square; the Harley–Cavendish family's Cavendish Square, with nearby Harley, Wimpole, Welbeck, Mortimer, and Portland Streets. The square was simply the Mediterranean "piazza" or "plaza" and was consciously imported by the fourth Earl of Bedford and Inigo Jones, whose Covent Garden, in the mid-seventeenth century, was the prototype of the others. (Because two sides of it were lined by an arcade, on which the front doors of the houses opened, the word "piazza" came to mean in English a porch or veranda.) In other cities the Royal Crescent and the Parades in Bath, and Merrion Square in Dublin are similar examples of artistically planned developments. All those mentioned were designed for occupancy by the wealthy; but even in domestic architecture intended for those of small means, eighteenth-century builders produced charming rows and terraces of well designed houses, unlike the mean and higgledy-piggledy constructions of the nineteenth and twentieth centuries.

There was also much construction of fine public buildings, particularly churches, a fact which must seem odd to those who think the century an age of religious indifference. Wren's great baroque St. Paul's Cathedral, completed in the reign of Anne, is of course the masterpiece; Wren is buried there, under the fine epitaph *Si monumentum requiris, circumspice*—"If you seek his monument, look around you." But Wren also built some fifty churches in the old City of London, which had been devastated by the Great Fire, churches with a dazzling diversity of lovely baroque steeples and splendid interiors—St. Clement Danes, St. Magnus Martyr, St. Stephen's, Walbrook, and the rest. Later, a Tory Parliament under Anne passed an act providing for the construction of another fifty churches in London and its environs, to take care of the expanding population. All of the fifty were by no means built, but among those that were were such lovely creations as James Gibbs' St. Mary-le-Strand, and Nicholas Hawksmoor's St. Mary Woolnoth and St. George's, Bloomsbury. Gibbs' St. Martin's-in-the-Fields was not erected under the Act of 1711, but from funds raised by the parish; its novel design of the façade of a Greek temple surmounted by a baroque spire became the model for innumerable New England churches. Every visitor to London and every student of the eighteenth century should become acquainted with the achievement of these men and of Thomas Archer, Henry Flitcroft, and other fine church architects.

Not too many of the important secular public buildings of London date from the eighteenth century—William Kent's Palladian Horse Guards, Sir William Chambers' Somerset House, and George Dance's Mansion House (the residence of the Lord Mayor) are the most important of those that survive. In the environs of London are Wren's fine Greenwich Hospital and additions to Hampton Court Palace. The university cities preserve fine baroque buildings in Wren's Sheldonian Theatre and Gibbs' Radcliffe Camera at Oxford, and Wren's library of Trinity College, Cambridge; and the public buildings of Dublin—Trinity College, the Four Courts, the Parliament House (later the Bank of Ireland), the latter two by James Gandon—make it architecturally one of the finest capitals in Europe.

The great architectural achievement of the age, however, was in "the stately homes of England"—the splendid variety of country seats of wealthy noblemen and successful merchants and politicians. As has been pointed out, important differences between the history of France and that of England may be traced to the fact that the French aristocracy tended to neglect their country estates and flock to the court of Versailles, whereas in England (then as now) everyone who could afford to do so seized any chance to flee into the country and stay there as long as possible: a seat in the country was the ultimate ambition of every City businessman. The fashion had begun long before, but the Prime Minister, Sir Robert Walpole, put his seal on it by pouring his questionably-got fortune into Houghton Hall, Norfolk (architect, Colin Campbell), and its magnificent collection of art.[7] Seats ranged in size and elaborateness from Sir John Vanbrugh and Nicholas Hawksmoor's grandiose Blenheim Palace, given by the nation to the great Duke of Marlborough, in gratitude for his military victories, Seaton Delaval, and Castle Howard, down to so unpretentious an establishment as that of Edmund Burke near Beaconsfield (eyebrows have been lifted about how an impecunious intellectual like Burke could have financed even it).

Many other affluent societies have built lavishly, but few with such artistic effectiveness as eighteenth-century Britain. The origins of its architecture can be traced to the early seventeenth century, when Inigo Jones, after visiting Italy and studying the work of the great Renaissance architects there, brought back to England a determination to make buildings that were not merely the rather shapeless functional masses of Tudor times but works of art, a joy to look at. His lovely Banqueting House (the scene of the execution of his patron, Charles I) still shines out amid a mass of uninspired civil service architecture in Whitehall. His great successor, Wren, a many-sided genius in the Renaissance tradition—he was a distinguished scientist as well as architect, President of the Royal Society and Savilian professor of astronomy at Oxford while still in his twenties—took the lessons of Italian Renaissance architecture equally to heart; his idol was Bernini. From it he evolved what may justly be called "English Baroque," which still gladdens the gray English skies in the ornate spires and façades of Wren's churches and those of his disciples, Hawksmoor, Vanbrugh, and Archer.

A reaction to this exuberance set in around the 1720's: as Sir John Summerson puts it, "Baroque architecture has always been a blind spot in English criticism. It is strange that, whereas the fantastic element in Swift was soon accepted as a golden thread in the literature of the time, the fantasy of Vanbrugh, Hawksmoor, and Archer has always been deeply suspect." [8] How suspect it was may be seen in the denunciations of it in Pope's *Epistle to Burlington.* Here Pope, who in *The Rape of the Lock* and *The Dunciad* could devise fantasies as vivid as anyone's, takes up the cudgels on behalf of his friend, the third Earl, who, with the assistance of the architect William Kent, had begun a crusade to "return to Palladio"—the great pioneer of Italian Renaissance architecture. Pope, Burlington, and Kent won an easy victory in an England always suspicious of too much imagination, and "Palladianism" became the officially accepted architectural idiom for several decades. The casual modern viewer would probably still instinctively classify it as baroque, but it does have a heavier, more restrained effect than that of Wren and his followers. A hostile critic might even call it pedantic, and it did originate in a kind of literalist devotion to what was thought to be the principles of Andrea Palladio (and, naturally, a falling off from the spirit of Palladio's own lively architecture). Even so, it is far less pedantic than mid-Victorian Gothic or much modern architecture.

Around the middle of the century, three new movements began, one only short-lived, though fascinating while it lasted, the other two of much longer duration. The first was the craze for "chinoiserie".[9] The idealization of China by Western Europe dates from the reports of the Jesuit missionaries in China, headed by Father Matteo Ricci, in the early seventeenth century, who gave the impression of a highly civilized and extremely artistic people from whom, indeed, Western Europeans could learn a great deal (Ricci was later subjected to severe criticism by his superiors for, in effect, having let himself be converted by the Chinese, instead of converting them). This notion was, of course, grist to the Deists' mills, proof that morality and "the good life," in every sense of the term, could subsist without the aid of institutionalized Christianity. By Bayle and others Confucius came to be regarded as at least as great a moral teacher as Jesus. The idea gave rise in literature to the popularity of the "oriental tale" and "oriental letters," in which Montesquieu, Voltaire, Goldsmith, Johnson, and others allowed exotic Eastern peoples to teach Europeans rational and virtuous behavior.

In art (helped, of course, by the expansion of trade), this craze gave rise to the fashions of collecting delicate Chinese porcelain, familiar to the readers of Pope and Wycherley, of using and imitating Chinese fabrics and wallpapers, to furniture of Chinese design (associated particularly with Chippendale), and the cult of the Chinese garden. The fashion was enthusiastically propagated by the architect Sir William Chambers (interestingly, with assistance from Johnson) in his *Designs of Chinese Buildings, Furniture, etc.,* 1757. Chambers attributes to the Chinese an aesthetic of asymmetry and contrast—"sharawadgi" it was termed according to Sir William Temple's earlier *Essay on Gardens.* Not much architecture on a large scale, of course, resulted from the fashion, except Chambers's famous pagoda in Kew Gardens, and parts of George IV's fantastic palace at Brighton, but in the minor decorative arts it has continued to flourish (happily) to the present day.

The other two movements, the Gothic and Classical revivals, were to have more spectacular effects. Gothic architecture had never lapsed completely in England. Wren worked in the Gothic idiom at Oxford, and the great west towers of Westminster Abbey, which most tourists automatically think of as equally medieval with the rest of the building, were in fact built by pupils of Wren in the 1730's and 1740's. But generally, of course, "Gothick" was despised as rude and tasteless. Its revival was the result partly of the awakening of interest by seventeenth and eighteenth-century scholars in the languages, literatures, and antiquities of medieval Europe, especially northern Europe—the work of such men as Milton's friend, Junius, George Hickes, Thomas Hearne, and Thomas Gray; and partly of Horace Walpole's indefatigable, and probably neurotic, championing of the obscure, the out-of-fashion, the underdog. Few buildings in history have been given such assiduous publicity as Walpole gave his gimcrack villa at Strawberry Hill, whose plaster battlements, it was said, had to be renewed every two or three years. But they and the other Gothic trappings did something for Walpole's insecure psyche (as did his similarly Gothic novel, *The Castle of Otranto,* the first of the flourishing genre of horror stories). Perhaps the full-fledged pseudo-Gothicism of the nineteenth century did something similar for that of the Victorians. Indeed, when one considers Walpole, and William Beckford's Gothic experiments at Fonthill, and, in the next century, the names of Pugin and Ruskin, one is struck by the extent to which the Gothic revival was a literary man's rather than an architect's invention.

In the middle of the eighteenth century, the excavation of the Greco-Roman cities of Herculaneum and Pompeii provided the impetus that was eventually to result in the Classical revival of the early nineteenth century (if the student of literature is bothered by the fact that in architecture this development is contemporary with Wordsworth and Shelley rather than with Pope and Swift, he would do well to reexamine his assumptions). Massive "Classical" domes and colonnades, like those of the British Museum, the National Gallery of London, University College, London, and countless nineteenth- and twentieth-century Capitols, Parliament buildings, court houses, and post offices were to dominate public architecture for another century or more almost as much as Gothic dominated ecclesiastical architecture.

Like Victorian Gothic, the revived Classical was an antiquarian, derivative idiom in which the chief concern was to duplicate ancient techniques, and which was ultimately sterile and boring. The impulse that gave rise to the architectural idiom of Wren, Vanbrugh, Kent, and the rest, on the contrary, though it can certainly be traced back, through Bernini and Palladio, to Vitruvius and Roman architecture, and hence is also sometimes called "classical," is so in a very different sense from what was produced by Smirke, Wilkins, and other early nineteenth-century Classical revivalists. In the Renaissance and eighteenth-century works, the classical sources have been used merely as a convenient base for the products of the architect's own fertile artistic imagination, and hence it is much better to distinguish it by use of the term "baroque." The best of those who worked after the rediscovery of Greek and Roman architecture in the mid-eighteenth century was certainly Robert Adam, who, like Palladio before him, used the discoveries merely as a stimulus for evolving his own peculiar and charming style. The failure of nerve, of confidence in the contemporary artistic imagination came later, and persisted throughout the nineteenth century and much of the early twentieth.

In the occupation of bringing into existence beautiful surroundings, the subsidiary arts of interior decorating and furniture making (Chippendale, Hepplewhite, Sheraton, the Adams) reached the highest level they have known in England. So did such minor, but appealing arts as those of woodcarving, in the hands of Grinling Gibbons, ornamental ironwork, by Jean Tijou, and ceramics, by the Wedgwoods and the Chelsea potters. But most interesting of all, as reflecting a change of sensibility, was that of landscape gardening, in which a great revolt took place against the formal, or symmetrical, garden which had been the ideal throughout the Renaissance and on the Continent. There may have been some nationalist feeling involved: the supreme example of formal landscaping had recently been completed by André Le Nôtre, at Louis XIV's palace of Versailles, and was the pride of France. Students taught to think of eighteenth-century England as dominated by "classical formalism" are always surprised to learn how vigorously the English intellectuals of the time, especially Pope and Addison, rejected the conception of the symmetrical garden in favor of the natural, or free-form, landscape. To be sure, it often proved very expensive and difficult to landscape the grounds of a country seat so that they would "resemble nature"—to replant trees in asymmetrical clumps, to keep up a costly natural lawn instead of covering the walks with gravel, to construct a "ha-ha"—a ditch containing a fence below eye level, so that one's eye could have a distant vista of a natural scene with grazing sheep and cows, but without the inconvenience that the close presence of these sometimes too natural creatures would bring. But Lancelot "Capability" Brown persuaded many noble landlords to sign his contracts—he got his nickname by solemnly viewing the unimproved grounds and presently pronouncing, "Well, my lord, I see a capability in it." His best known work is the extensive park surrounding Blenheim Palace, whose "naturalness" forms a piquant setting for the unabashed and exuberant "artificiality" of Vanbrugh's baroque masterpiece. No product of eighteenth-century English taste has had more enthusiastic a reception (a fact which may cause the cynic to wonder a little about its artistic soundness): "natural" landscaping has become virtually mandatory for parks and gardens throughout the world, with the exception of the Far East, and on the Continent a favorite name for a public park is *Englische Garten*.

Painting, Engraving, Sculpture

In music, it was noted above, a strong and healthy tradition of professionalism existed continuously in England from Tudor times onward, a tradition which was not overwhelmed by the importation of innovations from Italy or France, or by the powerful genius of a Purcell or Handel, but came easily and successfully to terms with them, contributing as much as it was contributed to. In architecture, such a native tradition did not exist (or, rather, the fine Gothic tradition that had flourished up to the fifteenth century had died out); but men like Jones and Wren and Hawksmoor and Adam were artists of sufficient genius to school themselves in the Renaissance Italian tradition and use it, not merely to make uninspired copies, but as the basis for genuinely original and imaginative work. In painting, however, it is hard to think of the name of a native English painter of any importance before the eighteenth century.[10] Patrons imported mature and established artists from the Continent—chiefly from the Netherlands—for a time to execute a series of commissions, after which they returned to their native land, their English visit a relatively unimportant episode in their careers: Hans Holbein in the reign of Henry VIII, Rubens and Van Dyck under the early Stuarts. Much the same situation existed after the Restoration, except that the immigrants—Lely, Kneller, Michael Dahl—arrived at an earlier age and stayed in England permanently.

It was not until the eighteenth century that an English tradition of painting developed. But when it did, it developed with remarkable speed and strength. This was no doubt another testimonial to the age's tremendous creative energy and power of assimilation and, of course, to the wealth which made large-scale portraits of individuals and families, and views of the family's holdings, a necessity for newly rich magnates to hang on the walls of their new country seats. First-rate portraitists like Reynolds soon became wealthy men themselves.

Perhaps the chief credit for launching the "English school" of painting should go to Jonathan Richardson the Elder, not a great painter, but an excellent theorist and propagandist: his *Essay on the Theory of Painting,* which he published in 1715 at the age of fifty, made a deep impression on both Hogarth and Reynolds; the profound humanism expressed in Reynolds' *Discourses* is earlier to be found in Richardson's *Essay*. Whatever the reasons for the phenomenon, the sudden appearance of a galaxy of fine painters is remarkable: Hogarth, one of a slightly older generation, was born in 1697, Allan Ramsay in 1713, Richard Wilson in 1714, Reynolds, Gainsborough, and Stubbs in the 1720's, Romney, Joseph Wright, Benjamin West, and John Singleton Copley (it seems reasonable to include these two immigrants from America) in the 1730's. Of the younger generation, usually thought of as "Romantic," or at least "Regency," Fuseli was born in 1741, Blake and Raeburn in the 1750's, Morland and Lawrence in the 1760's, Constable and Turner in the 1770's.

The giants of the group are unquestionably Hogarth, Reynolds, and Gainsborough—in what order, their admirers will continue to dispute. Hogarth is, of course, the odd man, the sport. Handicapped, as the later artists were not, by inadequate early instruction in draughtsmanship—to provide sound early technical instruction became one of the great objects of both Hogarth and Reynolds—he perhaps suffered from an unacknowledged feeling of inferiority, which made him combative and touchy. Always playing a lone hand, he refused to defer to the authority of the great Italian masters and their English disciples, and worked out his own unique idiom.

Thackeray (who had some training in art) was probably right in including Hogarth along with various literary figures in his *English Humorists:* there is a sense in which his work is literature rather than art; although his composition and color are most skillful, it is not his line that gives delight. About most artists, this would be a damning statement; but as a composer of literary works on canvas, Hogarth is so fine that the stricture seems hardly relevant. He himself fully recognized where his strength lay, and, engraving his most popular works for wide distribution, he set himself up as the pictorial recorder and reformer of contemporary English life, especially the seamier side of it. His sequences, "The Rake's Progress," "Marriage à la Mode," "The Harlot's Progress," are pictorial novels in miniature, distinguished, as novels should be, for their sharp and objective observation of the human scene, and their careful selection of detail so as to form a valid moral commentary on it. His portraits of individuals, especially of tough, hard-bitten men of the world, Lord Lovat, Bishop Hoadly, Captain Coram, spare their subjects nothing; yet the total effect is not one of shallow cynicism; they remain intensely human and sympathetic, and even that consummate crook, Lovat, becomes pitiable in his self-deception. With more sympathetic subjects—his servants, the cast of *The Beggar's Opera,* the Graham children— he is wonderfully compassionate and understanding, without ever falling into sentimentality. The lovely epitaph on him by Samuel Johnson does him justice:

> The hand of him here torpid lies,
>   That drew th' essential form of grace;
> Here clos'd in death th' attentive eyes,
>   That saw the manners in the face.

> If Genius warm thee, reader, stay,
>   If merit touch thee, shed a tear;
> Be Vice and Dulness far away;
>   Great Hogarth's honour'd dust is here.

Hogarth's satiric portraits of individuals who met his disapproval, such as John Wilkes and Charles Churchill, though clever, are not transcendently so. But in his satiric scenes of everyday life, "Morning," "Noon," "Evening," and "Night," "The Election," "A Modern Midnight Conversation," and the like, he adumbrated a technique of caricature that was to develop late in the century into the fantastically grotesque idiom of such masters as Rowlandson, Gillray, and Sayers, hardly surpassed in savagery and repulsiveness by Goya and Daumier. Again, innocent students who have been told of the restraint and decorum of the century are astonished, indeed appalled, when they first encounter Rowlandson's and Gillray's apocalyptic visions of human folly and degradation.

Reynolds's reputation among literary students (if what literary students think of his art is of any consequence) has suffered from the wide publicity given to Blake's hostile comments on him. But these have as little to do with the real Reynolds as Blake's similar comments on Johnson have to do with the real Johnson. Both names serve as symbols for Blake of something he dislikes; whether the men actually embody this is another question, to which the answer is very probably "No." The fact is, of course, that Reynolds' technical skill and artistic imagination are so self-evidently great that to attempt an apology would be presumption.

Like Handel (also a lifelong bachelor) Reynolds' devotion to his art above all else verged on the miraculous. Not even the Gordon Riots could interfere with his reaching his studio on time each morning; in the last decade of his long life, his niece complained, "My uncle seems more bewitched than ever with his palettes and pencils." He "went out" in society and contributed his share to the brilliant conversation of his and his friend Johnson's circle; yet, as one reads the passages about Reynolds in Boswell, one always senses a detachment which is not there in Johnson and Burke—the main part of his mind, one feels, is back at the studio, working on a difficult canvas.

Like other great artists—like his idol Michelangelo, whose name, with typically eighteenth-century dramatic effect, he contrived to stand as the last word he uttered as President of the Royal Academy—his art improved and deepened the older he became; such masterpieces as his paintings of Lord Heathfield and Archbishop Robinson come from the later years of his working life. As with Hogarth, his finest work was his portraits of active, experienced, mature, worldly men like these; as one critic puts it, "Reynolds's work may be seen as an equation between two great traditions—that of English character in the age of Marlborough and that of the master-periods of Italian painting." But, again like Handel, small samplings of his work do not do justice to Reynolds' dazzling fecundity: as the same critic says, "He of all painters most needs to be seen in the mass; only an overall view, and long perusal of examples taken from every period of his life, can give the measure of this giant professional." [11]

Portraiture, Reynolds' genre, was one of the two great styles of painting in which the age excelled. The other was the landscape. Humanity and the English countryside were the subjects which contemporary Englishmen most wanted to see represented on their walls. Reynolds' great rival, Gainsborough (to whom Reynolds paid a noble tribute in the *Discourse* delivered to the Royal Academy after Gainsborough's death) excelled in both. Much more the solitary, unsocial artist than Reynolds—he has even been described as Romantic—possessing none of Reynolds' deep sense of responsibility to English art and the English public, he eschewed academic life, painted as he pleased (and sometimes carelessly), declined honors, and died a much poorer man than Reynolds. (Yet George III much preferred him to Reynolds, and commissioned from him many charming portraits of the Royal Family.)[12] His portraits have an intimate quality often missing in those of Reynolds, especially when Reynolds thought it incumbent on him to be allegorical. The classic contrast is that between Reynolds' imposing picture of Mrs. Siddons, the great actress of the time, in all her glory, seated on a throne as "The Tragic Muse," and Gainsborough's portrait of her in a charming blue-and-white-striped afternoon dress, as the sweet and dignified English gentlewoman she was.

Of the three great landscape painters of the century, Richard Wilson, Gainsborough, and Constable (Constable's work, of course, extended well into the nineteenth century, but began in the eighteenth), it is hard to say which is the best. Their subjects were all the same—the landscape of southern England as Jane Austen described it:

> It was a sweet view—sweet to the eye and the mind. English verdure, English culture, English comfort, seen under a sun, bright without being oppressive.[13]

Wilson sometimes attempted more rugged scenes, such as the mountains of his native Wales; one of his finest pictures is that of Mount Snowdon, surprisingly Japanese in quality. Gainsborough's and Constable's landscapes everyone knows from numerous reproductions; Wilson was neglected in his own time and later, and his genius is perhaps only now beginning to be recognized.

That the best known works of all three are English subjects, however, by no means indicates an insular attitude toward their art. All of them studied the Dutch and Italian masters—Wilson spent six years in Italy, and painted much Italian landscape—and all of them were to some extent affected by the "romantic" influence of Claude Lorrain. At the other end of the scale, hints of the later techniques of the nineteenth-century French impressionists can be detected in the freer use of light and color in Constable's later work. As so often happened, the best in English art in the century was not the result of "untutored native genius" but of the imaginative assimilation of excellence of technique wherever it was to be found. For that matter, some of the finest English landscapes—or rather townscapes—of the century were painted by the Venetian Canaletto (nearly all of whose later production was purchased for George III by his consul in Venice, Joseph Smith, and is in the English royal collection). Canaletto was persuaded to come to England for some years, and his brilliant canvases of London and the Thames valley, with their vivid blue skies and shimmering light, are the best record available of the lovely eighteenth-century city that Wordsworth knew—"Earth has not anything to show more fair."

Eighteenth-century English painters, Reynolds included, felt uneasily that they had a duty to render "the sublime," which duty they usually fulfilled by turning out from time to time vast, crowded canvases depicting historical and allegorical scenes. They fail to impress us as they presumably impressed contemporaries (not that they impressed Samuel Johnson, who averred that he would rather have a portrait of a dog that he knew than the finest historical painting in the world; and it was Johnson, ahead of his time as usual, who sneered mightily at the use by moderns of hackneyed classical mythology). Certainly Reynolds' picture of an embarrassed-looking Garrick being dragged in opposite directions by the Muse of Tragedy and the Muse of Comedy tends only to make us smile. However, Benjamin West, an immigrant from Pennsylvania, made a huge success out of the genre (for instance, his "Death of Wolfe on the Plains of Abraham") and succeeded Reynolds as President of the Royal Academy.

There is much more that could be said about the riches of eighteenth-century British painting and engraving; Blake and his friend the Swiss immigrant Fuseli, in particular, call for discussion; but it is probably better to leave them for a later volume in this series. A final note, however, must call attention to an undeservedly neglected art that flourished during the century—that of sculpture, in particular portrait sculpture. Apart from Joseph Nollekens (and his father came from Antwerp), most of its practitioners were immigrants: Caius Gabriel Cibber (sculptor of the two famous statues of "Melancholy Madness" and "Raving Madness"—as we should now say, schizophrenia and paranoia—at the gate of Bedlam, which Pope felicitously termed his son Colley's "brazen, brainless brothers"), Louis François Roubiliac, John Michael Rysbrack. As with Reynolds' portraits (and Handel's music) what strikes one about their statues and busts—Nollekens' Handel and Johnson, Roubiliac's wonderful painted terra cotta bust of Colley Cibber, Rysbrack's Queen Caroline—is their subtle insight into human psychology and their immense dramatic energy. One is sometimes tempted to advance the thesis that the dramatic impulse in the eighteenth century, denied by censorship its legitimate expression on the stage, found its outlet in the other arts, in Handel's tremendous choral climaxes, Reynolds' arresting portraits, and the bold exaggeration of feature and expression in Roubiliac's and Nollekens' portrait sculpture.

A Note on Literary and Aesthetic Criticism and Theory

For many decades questions of eighteenth-century English artistic and literary taste and sensibility have usually been discussed in terms of two potent concepts, "neoclassicism" and "romanticism." A rough, but not too inaccurate, outline of the history of the English aesthetic from 1550 to 1850, as given in the great majority of literary histories from about 1870 onward, runs as follows: Three great movements can easily be discerned in the literary and artistic activity of the time, movements of, successively, action, reaction, then action again.[14] The English Renaissance, dated approximately 1550–1650 and centering on the reign of Elizabeth I, is characterized by boldness, adventurousness, and exuberant individualism, culminating in the great "irregular" drama and poetry of Shakespeare and the extravagant conceits of Donne. In 1660, however, as a result of the traumatic experience of the Civil War, men's minds recoiled, in literature as well as in politics, from such qualities, and sought order, decorum, regularity, and stability instead. The means by which these ends were achieved were two: first, an increased emphasis on the importance of the classical (chiefly Latin) writers, Horace, Virgil, and Juvenal in particular, as providing literary models, critical principles, and norms of social conduct for modern man; and, second, the reliance of artists and writers on rigid rules, such as the dramatic unities, for the composition of their works and a corresponding distrust of the imagination. The fact that Charles II and his court spent many years of exile at the French court before returning to England is credited with having assisted this process, influential French writers and critics of the time (Corneille, Racine, Boileau) having been infected with the neoclassical virus even earlier and more strongly.[15] Then in 1798 (though there had been foreshadowings in the shape of "pre-Romantics" such as Thomson, Gray, and the Wartons), *enfin Wordsworth vint,* along with Coleridge and Blake, to free the imagination from the shackles of these dead rules and models (and English literature lived happily ever after). To document the currency of such a picture from late nineteenth- and early twentieth-century textbooks of the history of English literature and criticism would be superlatively easy. One quotation will suffice here to illustrate it, the title of a lecture series given in the United States in 1884 by Edmund Gosse, *From Shakespeare to Pope: A History of the Decline of Romantic Poetry.*[16]

Childish as this sketch appears when presented thus baldly, and drastically as details of it have later been modified—it is encouraging to note that the concept of "pre-Romanticism," once accepted so unquestioningly, has been virtually abandoned by reputable modern literary historians[17]—its essential elements still hold a powerful sway over the minds of students. Yet it is salutary to observe how comparatively recently this pattern was imposed on the historical data.[18] The great writers of the eighteenth century, Dryden, Pope, Johnson (Swift has always been treated as an exception, sometimes even being termed a "Romantic" out of his time) were entirely unaware that they were "neoclassicists"; they did not use the term or any equivalent, nor is there any evidence that they thought of themselves as playing the role Arnold and others cast them in. Henry Hallam, in the earliest substantial literary history of the modern era, published between 1837 and 1839,[19] manages to make a thorough and perceptive survey of the literature of Europe, including England, between 1400 and 1700 without displaying any awareness of a shift from "Renaissance exuberance" to "neoclassical restraint." The history of the genesis and propagation of the concept of a "neoclassical age" needs thorough investigation. It seems safe to say, however, that it was mainly an invention of the obscure academics and journalists who, from around 1840 to 1870, wrote the pioneering textbooks of the new school subject of English literature, which was just being introduced into the curriculum of English and American colleges in the middle and late nineteenth century, and who felt a compulsion to provide a set of historical facts about the subject on which students could be examined. In short, the credentials of the concept are not so imposing that modern students need be frightened away from asking themselves whether, in spite of its wide currency, there is any compelling historical reason for accepting the hypothesis as valid.

This is not the place to enter into a detailed analysis of the question; but the student might usefully consider an alternative hypothesis that seems to fit the historical data at least as well as the "neoclassical" one—namely, that the eighteenth century, in England at least, far from representing a resurgence of reliance on previously abandoned classical rules and models, is, rather, the mid-point in a steady decline in reverence for the authority of the classical Latin and Greek writers, a decline which has been continuous from an apogee in the early Renaissance to the present, when the numbers of writers and critics who have any extensive first-hand acquaintance with the classics or regard them as in any way authoritative is small indeed. It is not surprising that Hallam failed to notice the occurrence of any "neoclassical" resurgence after 1660. He had recorded in detail that period in the early sixteenth century when "the real excellence of the ancients in literature as well as art gave rise to an enthusiastic and exclusive admiration of antiquity," the time when the test of a true intellectual was the ability to write "pure" Latin, "conformable to the standard of what is sometimes called the Augustan age, that is, of the period from Cicero to Augustus," [20] and, by comparison, the time of Dryden, Defoe, Bunyan, and Swift must have seemed a far cry indeed from such "exclusive admiration." He was aware of the great indebtedness to classical literature of earlier writers like Marlowe, Spenser, Ben Jonson, Donne, Milton, and Shakespeare himself—the fact is that allusions to the classics occur more frequently in Shakespeare's plays than in those of Dryden or in Pope's verse epistles or Johnson's essays. It is true that Dryden, Pope, and Johnson were writing for an audience who they assumed had the basic grounding in Latin literature that was the hallmark of every educated Englishman from the Renaissance down to the beginning of the twentieth century. It is also true that they enjoyed and admired Horace and Juvenal, and used them for their own purposes. But that the domination of Horace and Juvenal over the minds of eighteenth-century writers was greater than that of Seneca and Ovid over sixteenth-century writers, or that Dryden and Pope succumbed to their spell more than Shelley, say, to that of Aeschylus, or Tennyson to that of Virgil, or that either Dryden or Pope recommended the classical writers as guides for the moderns more strenuously than T. S. Eliot and Ezra Pound were later to do, would be difficult to prove. It was Pope who wrote, with sturdy independence, "Of One Who Would Not Be Buried in Westminster Abbey" (himself):

> Heroes and kings, your distance keep,
> In peace let one poor poet sleep,
> Who never flattered folks like you.
> Let Horace blush, and Virgil too.

It was Ezra Pound who wrote "Homage to Sextus Propertius."

Any study of eighteenth-century literary and aesthetic theory in England must begin by deciding for itself whether or not it will accept *a priori* the postulate that an aggressive neoclassicism (or its more fashionable modern synonym, "Augustanism") was the dominant intellectual pattern of the age. If any such study does, it will face many difficult problems when considering the work of the leading critics of the century, on which it will often have to render the verdict of "inconsistent" or "ambivalent," of wavering aimlessly between desire to adhere to the dominant theory and desire to rebel against it. Such a verdict has often been passed on both the century's greatest literary critic, Samuel Johnson, and its greatest art critic, Joshua Reynolds. The net result is to discredit their criticism, and indeed the whole body of criticism of the eighteenth century, as the work of men who fundamentally could not make up their minds, who lacked the courage of their critical convictions. If, on the other hand, they are seen as men who, though inheriting a residual legacy of authoritarianism and apriorism in critical matters from the Renaissance (which had in turn inherited it from the Middle Ages), nevertheless moved steadily and consistently in the opposite direction, and contributed greatly to the erosion of that legacy, such charges will fail. There will be no more need to be apologetic about these critics than there is about, say, another famous contemporary, Henry Cavendish, who, though reared in the medieval and Renaissance belief in the theory of phlogiston (a product, in the end, of Aristotelian physics) and never bringing himself to the point of formally renouncing this theory, nevertheless, by his "modern" experimentation with hydrogen and nitrogen, made immensely valuable contributions to the development of modern chemistry.

The fancied necessity of finding evidence in the writings of Johnson, Reynolds, and others to support the view that, at least part of the time, they were militant "neoclassicists," has frequently led to serious misreadings of their writings. Both Johnson and Reynolds were fond of using the term "general" as one of critical approbation.[21] Their modern expositors very often equate this with "abstract" and accuse them of preaching "abstractionism," though in fact Johnson never seems to have used "abstract" or "abstraction" as critical terms or said anything in favor of such a quality in imaginative writing. It is obvious, if one examines his texts without the presupposition that Johnson was a "neoclassicist," that by "general," as a term of approbation, he by no means meant "abstract." He illustrates his praise of Shakespeare's adherence to "general nature" by the example of King Claudius in *Hamlet,* and he makes it abundantly clear that it is not because Shakespeare's portrait of Claudius is an "abstract" representation of kingship that he admires it. On the contrary, he vigorously defends Shakespeare against the complaints of Voltaire and others that Claudius, in getting drunk, is much too *concrete,* too particularized, too little like the stereotype of a king. A little serious study of such passages soon convinces us that Johnson's position is precisely that of Ezra Pound when he praises Joyce's *Ulysses* and Eliot's *Prufrock:*

> James Joyce has written the best novel of the decade, and perhaps the best criticism of it has come from a Belgian who said, "All this is as true of my country as of Ireland." Eliot has a like ubiquity of application. Art does not avoid universals, it strikes at them all the harder in that it strikes though particularities. . . . [Eliot's] men in shirt-sleeves and his society ladies are not a local manifestation: they are the stuff of our modern world, and true of more countries than one.[22]

When Johnson praises "generality," he undoubtedly means "ubiquity of application" or "susceptibility of wide response," as no doubt Reynolds also does. And in the notorious passage in *Rasselas* where Imlac proclaims that the business of the poet is not to number the streaks of the tulips but "to exhibit . . . such prominent and striking features as recall the original to every mind," Johnson is surely saying no more than what Keats was later to say—that poetry should not surprise by "singularity; it should strike the reader as a wording of his own highest thoughts, and appear almost as a remembrance."

Indeed, the more one reads Johnson's remarks about how poetry should be written, the more strikingly his taste in poetry appears to resemble Wordsworth's. He detests archaic and contrived diction, the facile use of outworn mythology, unnatural inversion of normal English sentence order. Poetry, he thinks, should be communication among contemporary men in respect to contemporary issues and states of feeling, and its vehicle should be contemporary language. Gray's "images are magnified by affectation; the language is laboured into harshness. . . . His art and his struggle are too visible, and there is too little appearance of ease and nature"; Collins' "diction was often harsh, unskillfully laboured and unjudiciously selected. He affected the obsolete when it was not worthy of revival; and he puts his words out of the common order, seeming to think, with some later candidates for fame, that not to write prose is certainly to write poetry." [23] Johnson's objection to *Lycidas* is well summed up in Wordsworthian language—Milton's poem is patently *not* the spontaneous overflow of powerful feelings; and Johnson's own illustration of how an elegy should be written, "On the Death of Dr. Robert Levet," is a considerably Wordsworthian poem—even in its occasional descent into bathos, "His frame was firm, his powers were bright,/ Though now his eightieth year was nigh."

The critique of *Lycidas* is indeed an important crux in the assessment of Johnson's criticism, and to some degree of eighteenth-century criticism in general. After a century and a half of denigration, some students have begun to examine Johnson's critique seriously and to understand that, far from its being an expression of old-fashioned reactionism, it is a revolutionary document. One student has gone so far as to term it "the end of Renaissance criticism":

> Johnson was in several ways a "new man," a man of our sensibility rather than a man of the Renaissance. . . . Johnson . . . just as we today, was not very interested in the "kinds" of literature as such, and demanded that poetry accord with "nature," the accordance to be tested by "my surveys of life." He wanted genuine

passion in literature, and responded with passion to literature. He expected, as we expect, a funeral elegy to express the grief of the writer, not his adeptness at handling literary conventions; and at the end of his life, when he had lived much and suffered much, and forgotten nothing of the suffering, he found this desire for passion and above all for emotional truth in literature precisely in conflict with the Renaissance traditions which his education had affirmed. . . . Modern criticism begins with Johnson.[24]

Johnson's strictures on *Lycidas* are clarified by his two earlier *Rambler* essays on the pastoral *genre*. For him, the emotional effect of a pastoral poem comes from what we would call its realism—he defines it simply as "a poem in which any action or passion is represented by its effects upon a country life." The pastoral poetry of Theocritus and Virgil pleases him because it springs from their actual experience, in childhood and youth, of rural life in northern Italy and Sicily, and their nostalgic recollection of it after they have become city dwellers.[25] Later pastoral, like that of Spenser, Milton, and Pope, has failed because its writers have merely used a contrived rural setting as extrinsic ornament for declamation on current controversial political and religious questions, or an obituary of some recently deceased worthy, or simply to show off their own technical virtuosity; their shepherds are not countrymen whom they themselves have known, as Theocritus and Virgil did, but patently factitious stereotypes. Modern academic criticism rejects such an approach to the pastoral, and insists that we, as readers, accept it as an essentially artificial *genre* and train ourselves to sense the complex ironies implicit in the discrepancy between reality and illusion that it presents. But Johnson's ideal of the pastoral, though we may find it unacceptable, cannot be called reactionary or old-fashioned or, least of all, neoclassical. On the contrary, the ideal of presenting serious and universal human emotion in a realistic setting of "the simple life" is very modern. Crabbe, with Johnson's approval and assistance, would later attempt this; likewise Hardy, Frost, and many other late nineteenth- and early twentieth-century poets and novelists. It is a curious reflection that the work which Johnson's ideal of the pastoral most closely adumbrates is probably *Michael: A Pastoral Poem* (though he would also have approved of *The Death of*

the Hired Man), and there are close resemblances between what
is desiderated in *Ramblers* 36 and 37 and what is desiderated in
the Preface to *Lyrical Ballads*.

The point of this long preamble is primarily to suggest that,
much as eighteenth-century critical and aesthetic theory has
been studied by later scholars, the usefulness of such study has
too often been diminished by the attempt to fit the reading of
the century's critical texts into a preconceived framework of intellectual history. The modern student should certainly at
least try to approach the writings of eighteenth-century critics
and aestheticians without such preconceptions, and only later,
after he has familiarized himself with what these writers have
actually been saying, consider whether or not there is any need
to postulate such entities as "neoclassicism" and "Augustanism"
to explain it. This, at least, would have been the method recommended, as it was followed by a great many of those writers
themselves, products of a staunchly empiricist age. It is paradox-
ical, to say the least, that it has been by the exercise of a highly
aprioristic procedure that the criticism of that age has been stig-
matized as aprioristic.

That the century reveled in exploring the questions of what is
artistically effective and why is apparent when one notes the 225
titles of books on general literary and aesthetic theory published
between 1664 and 1800 which are listed in the *Cambridge Bibliography of English Literature,* followed by several hundred additional titles of works of criticism of particular genres and particular writers. "Dryden," said Johnson, "may be properly
considered the father of English criticism," and certainly the
contrast between the spotty and erratic history of English literary criticism before Dryden and the mighty proliferation of
critics and theorists after him is striking. It would be wrong
to try to explain this fact, as was once customary, by postulating an opposition between the creative imagination and
the critical spirit, and asserting that the quantity of criticism
produced by the eighteenth century is further proof that it was a
cool, judicious age of reason, which bridled and restrained the
soaring imagination—after all, as Eliot and others have pointed
out, some of the greatest English critics have also been some of

the greatest English poets. The phenomenon, on the contrary, is further proof of the century's exuberant curiosity, now ranging through scarcely explored territory, the complex operation of the human mind and emotions. Much of its critical effort was directed toward expanding taste, toward developing the reader's ability to respond to a wider range of literature—the difficult poetry of the politically unpopular Milton (Dryden and Addison), that of Chaucer (Dryden), the folk ballads (Addison and Percy—whom Johnson helped in preparing the *Reliques* for the press), Hebrew poetry (Lowth), Norse literature (Gray and others), the medieval romances, and Renaissance narrative poetry deriving from them, such as that of Spenser, Ariosto, and Tasso (Hurd), Middle English literature (Thomas Warton), above all Shakespeare, the modern editing of whose works begins with Rowe in 1709. As for cautious reliance on classical authority, Dryden himself may be said to have promulgated the century's declaration of critical independence in his splendid assertion, " 'Tis not enough that Aristotle has said so, for Aristotle drew his models of tragedy from Sophocles and Euripides; and *if he had seen ours, might have changed his mind.*" [26]

In the short space of the present volume, there is no room to attempt even a summary of the century's vast production of "Essays on Criticism," "Essays on Taste," "Essays on Design," "Essays toward Fixing the True Standards of Wit," "Dissertations on Genius," "Observations on Style," and the like. Of course it may well be asked how useful it is to the student of the imaginative literature of the time to familiarize himself with all these—to what extent they will sharpen his understanding and appreciation of the literature itself. Much of this critical and aesthetic theorizing was written by men who were not greatly skilled, if at all, in any of the arts: Lord Kames, for instance, was a judge of the Scottish courts of justice, Alexander Gerard and Hugh Blair Presbyterian divines, Archibald Alison a Scottish Episcopalian divine (one wonders why theorizing about the nature of beauty should have so appealed to Scottish clergymen, of all people). And even when such theorizing is undertaken by a practitioner of the arts, it is an old truism that, as Coleridge observed of Wordsworth, his theory may give by no means an accurate report of his practice. An outstanding eighteenth-century illustration of this is Hogarth, who was very proud of the theory evolved in his *Analysis of Beauty* that an S-shaped curve of certain proportions ("the line of beauty") is the essential component of all artistically excellent design. But it has been pointed out that such a curve is preeminently characteristic of the rococo, which Hogarth detested, and it would be a hopeless task to try to locate the excellencies of Hogarth's own art in his use of the "line of beauty."

Aesthetics is, of course, a branch of philosophy or psychology, and the most fruitful contributions to a satisfactory theory of aesthetics were made by philosophers, or rather psychologists in the guise of philosophers, as most of the great eighteenth-century British philosophers were. If Dryden was the father of English criticism, Locke was certainly the father of eighteenth-century English aesthetic theory. Locke's great service was to reject the old Greek theory that the human mind works with inherent "logic," and to propound instead the theory of "associationism"—that we think and feel what we do largely as a result of the fortuitous associations provided by our past experience of the things we see, hear, touch, taste, and smell. A child sees a cane and trembles, not because of any logical reasoning about the nature of canes, but because in the past it has been applied vigorously to his bottom; conversely, when he sees a bon bon, he smiles. Berkeley, especially in his *New Theory of Vision,* and David Hartley, in his *Observations on Man,* push this Pavlovianism even farther; and David Hume comes to the conclusion that all "reasoning" is simply habit, the product of "conditioning" by experience. As for aesthetics, Hume declares, "Beauty is no quality in things themselves: it exists merely in the mind which contemplates them; and each mind perceives a different beauty." The simple existential act of liking or disliking comes first; afterward we try to work out a rationale to explain our doing so. That there was a nexus between such empiricist aesthetics and the practical criticism of the time is evident when we consider such a passage as Johnson's "general observation" on *Julius Caesar* (and Johnson professed no admiration of Hume): "Of this tragedy," he begins, "many particular passages deserve regard, and the contention and reconcilement of Brutus and Cassius is universally celebrated." "But," adds Johnson coolly,

"*I have never been strongly agitated in perusing it,* and think it somewhat cold and unaffecting," and this is enough to damn the work as far as Johnson is concerned.

Aesthetic theorists of the eighteenth century tend to be divided into two main classes, those who in the main concur with Locke and Hume and seek to find the causes of our liking or disliking something in the history of human experience, and those who, on the contrary, adhere to pre-Lockian psychology and postulate an "innate sense" in man which intuitively turns toward what is, in the nature of things, inherently and absolutely beautiful. The second group is not large, but a few influential eighteenth-century writers, notably Shaftesbury and, less dogmatically and more intelligently, Francis Hutcheson, stick to their Platonic guns and insist on the innate aesthetic sense which automatically responds to the true, the beautiful, and the good. The vast majority of English theorists and critics of the period fall, however, into the first category. There is Addison, whose *Spectator* essays on the imagination take an essentially psychological approach. There is Johnson, who shrewdly points out, among many other things, that the "unities" of time and place in the drama have no psychological justification, since the imagination of the spectator can quite as easily transfer him from Rome to Alexandria in the middle of a play as it transferred him from a hard theater seat in London to Rome at the beginning of it, and (in *Rambler* 60) that the source of the pleasure one gets from reading fiction or biography is what we should now call empathy. There is Burke, who finds that we are moved by "the sublime" (objects characterized by vastness, obscurity, a sense of power, and the like) when we have an "idea" of pain and danger without actually experiencing them, by contrast with our reaction to "the beautiful," whose characteristics are smallness, smoothness, delicacy, and so on. There is Lord Kames, who, though he begins by assuring us that taste is innate, nevertheless goes to great lengths to explain in associationist terms *why* some things are beautiful and others not (when you erect a "ruin" in your garden, be sure to construct it in Gothic rather than Greek style, because a Gothic ruin brings associations of time triumphing over strength, a melancholy but not unpleasing thought, whereas a Greek ruin represents the

triumph of barbarity over taste, a gloomy and discouraging reflection). There are Hugh Blair (a stream running safely between banks is beautiful; a waterfall is sublime) and Archibald
Alison, who is perhaps the most thoroughgoing associationist of
them all—anything, he thinks, can be made affecting by associa-
tion; there was, he tells us, a mathematician whose blood ran
cold and whose hair stood on end when he read Newton's *Optics;*
"The call of a goat among rocks," he says, "is strikingly beautiful, as expressing wildness and independence; in a farmyard,
not so."

As interesting as all this may be to the student of the intellectual history of the time, it may be questioned whether much of
it is actually relevant to the art of the Restoration and eighteenth century and the delight and instruction which that art is
capable of affording to the modern listener, viewer, and reader.
The truly great critics of the age, Dryden, Johnson and Reynolds, are also, as often happens, great executants of the arts they
discuss; and Dryden and Johnson are much more critics than
"metacritics"—they are concerned primarily with the concrete
work before them, and very little with weaving grandiose generalizations about how the beautiful is to be defined. Reynolds, to
be sure, in the fifteen presidential *Discourses* he delivered to the
Royal Academy, tends to generalize more: it is a tendency
inherent in the *genre* of the "presidential address," whether delivered to a gathering of artists, businessmen, university grad-
uands, or even philological scholars.

Reynolds' *Discourses* have had an unenthusiastic reception
for some time, largely, perhaps, because of Blake's witty aphorisms jotted in the margins of his copy of them. Yet the more one
reads Reynolds, the more one is impressed by the seriousness
and insight and the maturity and the *rightness* of so much of
what he has to say. It becomes clear, for instance, as one studies
the *Discourses* thoughtfully, that Reynolds is no more guilty
than his friend Johnson of the most damning error that is
charged against them both, that of advocating "generality," in
the sense of "abstractness," in art: they are as well aware as
Blake and Ezra Pound that the material of art is particularities,
whatever the effect on the audience may be.[27] And after so much
elaborate theorizing in a vacuum, which lesser critics of the

eighteenth century (as in other centuries) were so fond of indulging in, it is reassuring to be told by Reynolds, in his thirteenth *Discourse,*

> All theories which attempt to direct or control the Art, upon any principles falsely called rational, which we form to ourselves upon supposition of what ought in reason to be the end or means of Art, independent of the known first effect produced by the objects on the imagination, must be false and delusive.

It is clear that the greatest critics of eighteenth-century England were no more under the spell of "reason" than were its greatest philosophers and greatest poets.

NOTES TO CHAPTER FOUR

1. *Studies in Oxford History, Chiefly in the Eighteenth Century* (Oxford: Oxford Historical Society, 1901), p. 28.

2. *Brideshead Revisited* (Boston: Little, Brown, 1945), p. 82.

3. Article "Architecture: Modern Architecture."

4. Margaret Whinney and Oliver Millar, *English Art, 1625–1714* (Oxford: The Clarendon Press, 1957), p. 1.

5. Perhaps it is its Welsh (Tudor) ancestry that accounts for the strong musical tradition of the British royal family, from Henry VIII, who composed songs, down through the Georges, with their devotion to Handel, and Queen Victoria, proud of having studied singing under Mendelssohn and a fine patron of contemporary music, to George V's grandson, the Earl of Harewood, a music critic and director of the Edinburgh Festival.

6. A slight break in the continuity occurred during the 1640's and 1650's, when the Puritans frowned on elaborate liturgy, and the choir of the Chapel Royal was temporarily disbanded. Yet music did not suffer as theater did. No major writer has ever been a more devoted lover of music than Milton, the son of a not undistinguished composer of madrigals and motets. Indeed, the Puritan regime has been credited with having been favorable to the development of opera, since the ban on stage plays did not extend to dramatic performances with music.

7. Although Pope and others berated Walpole as indifferent, even hostile, to the arts, the great Houghton collection was one of the finest of the time. It had a curious later history: Walpole's grandson, the third Earl of Orford, sold it to Catherine the Great of Russia, who was then assembling the Hermitage collection; then in the 1920's, the Soviet government, pressed for money, sold important pieces from the collection to Andrew Mellon, who added them to the new National Gallery of Art in Washington. Thus the great eighteenth-century Prime Minister's collection

172   THE AGE OF EXUBERANCE

helped to provide the nucleus for the national collections of two great
world powers of the twentieth century.

Eighteenth-century British politicians seemed, in general, to choose
more impressive avocations than many of their successors. Walpole's great
rival, Robert Harley, Earl of Oxford, and his son were great collectors of
books and manuscripts: the Harleian Miscellany, the catalogue of the
Harleian Library (on both of which Samuel Johnson was employed), and
the Harleian collection of manuscripts in the British Museum testify to
the importance of their work. On a somewhat lower intellectual level,
Godolphin, Lord Treasurer under Queen Anne, was the founding father
of modern British horse racing and imported the famous Godolphin
Arab, ancestor of all British thoroughbreds; Lord Townshend's important
services to agriculture have already been noted in Chapter One.

8. *Georgian London* (London: Pleiades Books, 1945), p. 78.

9. William W. Appleton, *A Cycle of Cathay* (New York: Columbia University Press, 1951), is an excellent account of the history of the movement.

10. Two exceptions are the mysterious Nicholas Hilliard, painter of
miniatures in the reign of Elizabeth, and William Dobson, painter of
portraits in the earlier seventeenth century.

11. John Russell, "British Portrait Painters," in W. J. Turner, ed.,
Aspects of British Art (London: Collins, 1947), pp. 133–135.

12. The King may have objected, as some Johnsonians do to Reynolds'
portraits of Johnson, that Reynolds fictionalized his subjects excessively.
Reynolds is nearly as much responsible as Boswell for making Johnson
into a quaint, eccentric, laughable figure ("Mr. Oddity"). The noble portrait of Johnson by Opie does more justice than any of Reynolds' to the
grave, tender, sensitive, and deeply compassionate man that emerges from
many of Johnson's writings—for instance, the elegy on the death of Dr.
Levet.

13. *Emma*, Chapter 42.

14. It is probably no coincidence that this notion began to achieve currency around the same time as Macaulay's version of the Victorian theory
of inevitable human progress: "We have often thought that the motion
of the public mind in our country resembles that of the sea when the
tide is rising. Each successive wave rushes forward, breaks, and rolls back;
but the great flood is steadily coming on" (essay on Sir James Mackintosh). This was published in 1825, but of course it was not until some
decades later that Macaulay's writings, in cheap editions, reached their
widest audience. Macaulay and his fellow Whig politicians, as well as
disseminating such historical cheer, also dabbled in literary criticism,
generally with unfortunate results.

15. And of course this is a libel on the great French literature of the
seventeenth century. Lytton Strachey brilliantly points out (in *Landmarks in French Literature*, Oxford University Press, 1912) how in Racine
the observation of the unities effects a compression, an almost unbearable
intensity of passion seldom achieved in English drama.

16. Gosse, *America: The Diary of a Visit, Winter 1884–1885*, R. L. Peters
and D. G. Halliburton, eds. (West Lafayette, Indiana: Department of
English, Purdue University, 1966), p. iii.

17. "What does the best verse of Coleridge, Landor, Keats, Shelley, and even Wordsworth and Byron derive from the pre-Romantics? . . . Only in a very general sense can 'Tiger, tiger, burning bright,' 'The Solitary Reaper,' and the 'Ode to a Nightingale' be rendered as the flowering of the poetry of Dyer, Thomson, the Wartons, Gray, and Collins": Raymond D. Havens, "Discontinuity in Literary Development: The Case of English Romanticism," *Studies in Philology,* XLVII (January 1950), p. 103.

18. The earliest listing of "neo-classic" in the *Oxford English Dictionary* —though, to be sure, in a very sketchy treatment—is 1881.

19. *Introduction to the Literature of Europe in the Fifteenth, Sixteenth, and Seventeenth Centuries.*

20. Hallam, I, 315–316 (2nd ed., 1843).

21. On the other hand, when Johnson uses the term "general" as one of denigration—as he frequently does—he *is* clearly using it in the sense of "abstract": e.g., of Rowe, "I know not that there can be found in his plays any deep search into nature, any accurate discriminations of kindred qualities, or nice display of passion in its progress: all is general and undefined."

22. *Instigations* (New York, 1920), p. 199; originally published in *Poetry* (Chicago), 1917.

23. After a long period in which much confusion was caused by critics who seemed to postulate that there was one language for prose and a different one for poetry, T. S. Eliot returned to the position of Johnson (and Wordsworth): "Certain qualities are to be expected of any type of good verse at any time; we may say the qualities which good verse shares with good prose. . . . One does not need to examine a great deal of the inferior verse of the eighteenth century [or any other century, one might add] to realize that the trouble with it is that it is not prosaic enough. . . . To have the virtues of good prose is the first and minimum requirement of good poetry" (Introduction of Haslewood Books edition of *London* and *The Vanity of Human Wishes,* 1930).

24. Oliver F. Sigworth, "Johnson's *Lycidas:* The End of Renaissance Criticism," *Eighteenth-Century Studies,* I (December 1967), 166–168. See also Warren L. Fleischauer, "Johnson, *Lycidas,* and the Norms of Criticism," in *Johnsonian Studies,* Magdi Wahba, ed. (Cairo, 1962).

25. "Theocritus came here [to Alexandria] late in his career. He had been born at Cos and had lived in Sicily, and he arrived full of memories that no town-dweller could share—memories of fresh air and the sun, of upland meadows and overhanging trees, of goats and sheep, of the men and the women who looked after them, and of all the charm and the coarseness that go to make up country life. He had thrown these memories into poetical form": E. M. Forster, *Alexandria: A History and a Guide* (New York: Doubleday [Anchor Books], 1961: originally published 1922), p. 35. In considering Johnson's fondness for the "authentic" pastoral of Theocritus and Virgil, it might be remembered that he too, like them, had been a country, or at least small town, dweller until he moved to the metropolis at the age of twenty-eight. Spenser, Milton, and Pope, on the other hand, were all native Londoners.

26. John Dryden, "Heads of an Answer to Rymer," written *ca.* 1678. It was Johnson who first publicized the work, printing it from Dryden's holograph, owned by Garrick, in his *Life of Dryden*.

27. Blake's most famous piece of marginalia on Reynolds is regularly garbled. It is usually reported as follows:

> "This disposition to abstractions, to generalizing and classification, is the great glory of the human mind" (Reynolds). "To generalize is to be an idiot. To particularize is the alone distinction of merit. General knowledges are those knowledges that idiots possess" (Blake).

If the source (the 1798 edition of the *Discourses*) is consulted, it will be seen that Reynolds wrote nothing of the kind. Blake's comment is on a statement attributed by Edmond Malone to Burke. Reynolds was as well aware as Blake that the achievements of the human mind which he admired most greatly were composed not of "abstractions" but of very concrete blobs and streaks of paint.

Perhaps the most perceptive treatments of Reynolds as critic that have been published are Hoyt Trowbridge, "Platonism and Sir Joshua Reynolds," *English Studies*, XXI (1939), 1–7, and Harvey D. Goldstein, "*Ut Poesis Pictura:* Reynolds on Imitation and Imagination," *Eighteenth-Century Studies*, I (Spring 1968), 213–235.

BIBLIOGRAPHICAL NOTE

I. GENERAL BIBLIOGRAPHY

The resources for the study of this complex period are so rich and varied that few readers will wish to confine themselves to the handful of works of which limited space permits mention in this note. As a guide to further reading, two bibliographical pamphlets by James L. Clifford, *Early Eighteenth-Century Literature* (revised, 1962) and *Later Eighteenth-Century Literature* (revised, 1960) distributed by the Columbia University Bookstore, New York, are recommended. They provide an excellently arranged selective list, not merely of literary texts and criticism, but of "background" works as well. The standard annual bibliography of the period, "English Literature, 1660–1800," appearing in *Philological Quarterly* each July, also provides admirable coverage of background material in political, social, ideological, and aesthetic history. The bibliographies from 1925 to 1960 have been accumulated and published in four volumes by the Princeton University Press.

II. SOCIAL HISTORY

The most useful single work for the student who wishes an accurate knowledge of the way of life in eighteenth-century Britain is A. C. Turberville (ed.), *Johnson's England,* 2 vols. (Oxford: Clarendon Press, 1933). It is a collection of 27 fascinating essays on various aspects of eighteenth-century life by experts in the field—e.g., "The Church" by Norman Sykes; "The Navy" by Admiral Sir Herbert Richmond; "The Army" by Sir John Fortescue; "London" by Dorothy George; "Architecture and the Garden" by Geoffrey Webb; "Sculpture" by Katherine Esdaile; "The Law" by Sir Frank Mac-Kinnon; book publishing by R. W. Chapman; "The Newspaper" by D. Nichol Smith. The value of the work is enhanced by 158 illustrations. A less sumptuous but still useful attempt to give a similar view is A. C. Turberville, *English Men and Manners in the Eighteenth Century* (London: Oxford University Press, 1926). Shorter but more up-to-date accounts are given by J. H. Plumb, *England in the Eighteenth Century* (Penguin Books, 1950) and Dorothy Marshall, *English People in the Eighteenth Century* (London: Longmans, 1956).

Still a classic, and delightful reading in spite of its prejudice, is the famous Chapter Three of Macaulay's *History of England* (1849), "The State of England in 1685." It is a curious paradox that for all Macaulay's and Thackeray's Victorian censure of eighteenth-century morality, they were obviously fascinated by the exuberance of the age and appreciative of it. If the modern reader can bring himself to ignore their moralizing, no more vivid introduction to the eighteenth century can be found than Macaulay's essays dealing with the period—e.g., those on Addison, Johnson, Horace Walpole, Fanny Burney, the two Pitts—and Thackeray's *Henry Esmond, The English Humorists,* and *The Four Georges.*

III. POLITICAL HISTORY

There is a great need for an up-to-date, single-volumed political history of Britain in the Restoration and eighteenth century (Dorothy Marshall's *Eighteenth Century England* [London: Longmans, 1963] is much more a social than a political history). For the period 1714–1800, the most useful single work at present available is probably V. H. H. Green, *The Hanoverians* (London: Edward Arnold, 1948). It incorporates some of the revolutionary findings of the modern school of historians of the time, led by Sir Lewis Namier, whose *The Structure of English Politics at the Accession of George III* (London: Macmillan, 1929) was the opening blast in the destruction of the older Victorian or "Whig" interpretation, exemplified in the work of Lord Macaulay, J. R. Green, W. E. H. Lecky, and G. M. Trevelyan. J. Steven Watson, *The Reign of King George III, 1760–1815* (Oxford: Clarendon Press, 1960), a volume in the Oxford History of England, is unhesitatingly recommended. J. H. Plumb, *The First Four Georges* (London: Batsford, 1956) is an amusing and, on the whole, sympathetic account of the royal family of the time. Some more specialized works are Sir Lewis Namier's essays on George III, "Monarchy and the Party System," and the "country gentlemen," in his *Personalities and Powers* (London: Hamish Hamilton, 1955); Richard Pares, *King George III and the Politicians* (Oxford: Clarendon Press, 1953); John B. Owen, *The Rise of the Pelhams* (London: Methuen, 1957); Archibald S. Foord, *His Majesty's Opposition, 1714–1830* (Oxford: Clarendon Press, 1964); J. H. Plumb, *Sir Robert Walpole* (London: Cresset, 1956–1960), 2 vols. published of a projected 3 vols.

IV. INTELLECTUAL HISTORY

No seriously comprehensive attempt to trace the controlling ideas of British thought in the eighteenth century exists, although there are studies of certain individual movements and aspects. The title of Sir Leslie Stephen's *English Thought in the Eighteenth Century* (London: Smith, Elder, 1876) is a misnomer: it is a lively and searching study of the work of a number of writers of the time, including that of the best known Deists. But there was much more to "English thought" of the time than this; moreover, when Stephen has to deal with orthodox Christian teaching, as he frequently does, it is with the bias of a militant agnostic. Basil Willey, *The Eighteenth Century Background* (London: Chatto and Windus, 1940) manages to be at the same time over-specialized and superficial. A. O. Lovejoy, *The Great Chain of Being* (Cambridge, Mass.: Harvard University Press, 1936) is a brilliant study of the history and implications of the idea of the "Great Chain," which certainly had much influence on certain Renaissance and seventeenth-century English writers. It would be wrong, however, to infer, as some students seem to have done—though Lovejoy nowhere justifies the inference—that it was widely influential in the eighteenth century. The conclusions of some recent books by literary students which attempt a facile synthesis of the "sensibility of the eighteenth century" in a simple phrase or two should be viewed with great caution.

A serious student of the thought of the time should certainly familiarize himself with British empiricist philosophy. Locke, Ber-

keley, and Hume prided themselves (unlike Continental philosophers) on writing in lucid colloquial prose, easily comprehensible
by the ordinary educated reader, and the best introduction to their
philosophy is through their own writings. The racy chapters dealing
with the movement in Bertrand Russell's *History of Western Philosophy* (New York: Simon and Schuster, 1945), himself sympathetic
to the empiricists and the tradition of "easy writing" in philosophy,
are perhaps as good a "survey" as any for the modern student; but
for something more solemn, he may consult W. R. Sorley, *A History
of British Philosophy* (New York and London: Putnam, 1921), an
expansion of Sorley's chapters on the subject in the *Cambridge
History of English Literature*. Nor should he neglect the history
of science during the period: Marjorie Nicolson's studies, such as
Science and Imagination (Ithaca, New York: Cornell University
Press, 1956) and *Mountain Gloom and Mountain Glory* (Cornell
University Press, 1959), treat its impact on the creative imagination
of the time.

There is no adequate account for the modern reader of what,
doctrinally, Christianity in eighteenth-century Britain meant. Norman Sykes' *Church and State in Eighteenth-Century England*
(Cambridge: Cambridge University Press, 1934) is a brilliant study
of the Church of England in its temporal relations, which destroys
the myth of its "stagnation" during this period. Bishop Stephen
Neill's *Anglicanism* (Penguin Books, 1958) is a useful introduction
for the beginner. But perhaps the best course for the student who
wants to know the significance of Anglicanism for the eighteenth
as well as other centuries is to familiarize himself with the contents
of the Book of Common Prayer.

V. ARTISTIC AND AESTHETIC HISTORY

There are a number of excellent recent histories of British painting,
sculpture, and architecture during the period—the relevant volumes of the Oxford History of Art (Oxford: Clarendon Press) and
the Pelican History of English Art (Penguin Books), Sir John Summerson, *Georgian London* (London: Pleiades Books, 1945) and Sir
Albert Richardson, *An Introduction to Georgian Architecture* (London: Art and Technics, 1949). There are also skillful recent studies
of many individual artists, such as those of Hogarth by Ronald
Paulson (New Haven: Yale University Press, 1965), Richard Wilson
by W. G. Constable (London: Routledge and Kegan Paul, 1953),
William Kent by Margaret Jourdain (London: Country Life, 1948),
James Gibbs by Bryan D. G. Little (London: Batsford, 1955), and

Nicholas Hawksmoor by Kerry Downes (London: Zwemmer, 1959). There is a large literature on landscape gardening of the time (e.g., Ralph Dutton, *The English Garden* [London: Batsford, 1937]) and on other minor arts, such as interior decorating and furniture-making. W. W. Appleton, *A Cycle of Cathay* (New York: Columbia University Press, 1951) is an excellent historical account of the fashion of *chinoiserie*.

Modern appreciation of English music of the baroque age is not yet as fully developed as that of the visual arts or Continental baroque music; the standard histories (e.g., *The Oxford History of Music*, Vol. IV [Oxford: Clarendon Press, 1902; 2nd ed., 1931]) still carry a large content of Victorian and romantic suspicion of it. Perhaps the best modern study unhampered by such limitations is Paul Henry Lang's monumental *George Frideric Handel* (New York: Norton, 1966). The short volumes on Purcell by Sir Jack Westrup (1937) and Handel by E. J. Dent (1934) in the "Master Musicians" series (London: Dent; New York: Dutton) are also useful.

A convenient source-book for eighteenth-century aesthetic and literary theory is Scott Elledge (ed.), *Eighteenth-Century Critical Essays*, 2 vols. (Ithaca, New York: Cornell University Press, 1961).

✣ Index

Abbreviations: Abp = Archbishop; Bp = Bishop; Css = Countess; Mss = Marquess; Pss = Princess; Vct = Viscount.

The notes and chronological tables have not been indexed.